Early Business Contacts

GW01003421

Other ESP titles of interest include:

ADAMSON, D.
International Hotel English*

BINHAM, P. *et al.*
Hotel English*

BINHAM, P. *et al.*
Restaurant English*

BLAKEY, T.
English for Maritime Studies (second edition)*

BRIEGER, N. and J. Comfort
Business Contacts*

BRIEGER,N. and A. Cornish
Secretarial Contacts*

BRIEGER, N. and J. Comfort
Technical Contacts*

BRIEGER, N. and J. Comfort
Social Contacts*

BRIEGER, N. and J. Comfort
Business Issues

DAVIES, D. and D. Pickett
Preparing for English for Commerce

DAVIES, S. *et al.*
Bilingual Handbooks of Business Correspondence and Communication

KEANE, L.
International Restaurant English*

McGOVERN, J. and J. McGovern
Bank on Your English*

PALSTRA, R.
Telephone English*

PALSTRA, R.
Telex English

POTE, M. *et al.*
A Case for Business English*

ROBERTSON, F.
Airspeak*

* includes audio cassette(s)

Early Business Contacts

Materials for developing listening and speaking skills for the student of Business English

Nick Brieger and Jeremy Comfort

ENGLISH LANGUAGE TEACHING
Prentice Hall

New York   London   Toronto   Sydney   Tokyo   Singapore

First published 1989 by
Prentice Hall International (UK) Ltd,
66 Wood Lane End, Hemel Hempstead,
Hertfordshire, HP2 4RG
A division of
Simon & Schuster International Group

Printed and bound in Great Britain at
the University Press, Cambridge
Reprinted with corrections 1989

Library of Congress Cataloging-in-Publication Data

Brieger, Nick.
   Early business contacts/Nick Brieger &
   Jeremy Comfort.
      p.   cm.
   Includes index.
   ISBN 0-13-222357-0. $8.00 (est.)
    1. Business communications — Study and
teaching. 2. English language — Business
English — Study and teaching. I. Comfort,
Jeremy. II. Title.
HF5718.873   1989
001.54 — dc19   88-37301
                            CIP

British Library Cataloguing in Publication Data

Brieger, Nick, *1948–*
   Early business contacts.
   1. English language. Business English. For
non-English speaking secretaries
   I. Title   II. Comfort, Jeremy
808'06665'1021

ISBN 0-13-222357-0

---

10 9   8 7 6 93

To Anna, Lisa and Daniel

Contents

The contents list below indicates the **topic themes** for each unit on the left, followed by the **language area or skill**.

Introduction

Targets and Objectives

This book is aimed at students who have a professional need for Business English; people either in, or training for, jobs in the business world.

More specifically, the material is relevant for learners, at pre-intermediate level or above, who need revision or further practice in developing listening skills for:

1. extracting relevant information
2. structuring information
3. inferring meaning from context
4. becoming accustomed to different varieties of English.

The material also develops speaking skills through:

1. problem-solving activities
2. role-plays
3. discussion topics

Organisation of Material

There are 25 units in the first part of the book (see Contents page). Each unit consists of:

1. Listening

A taped listening passage, accompanied by an information task.

2. Presentation

Highlighting and explanation of language items from the listening passage.

3. Controlled practice

Exercises designed to give practice in the language items introduced in the Presentation.

4. Transfer

Pair work, or occasionally group work, designed to encourage students to use the language introduced and practise it in a freer context.

5. Word check

A glossary of the business vocabulary that appears in the listening passage.

The second part of the book contains the Key Section for each unit. This includes:

Listening (1)

A tapescript and answers to the listening task.

Controlled practice (3)

Answers to the controlled practice exercises.

Transfer (where necessary) (4)

Information for pair work activities.

The **Vocabulary Index** at the back of the book provides an alphabetical list of all words which appear in the unit glossaries (Word Check) together with the unit numbers of their appearances.

The **Telex Appendix** provides a list of telex short forms together with their expanded forms.

The Roles of Teacher and Student

The materials provide the teacher with an opportunity to strike a balance between two classroom roles: teacher-controlled and teacher-monitored.

They also give students an opportunity for autonomous learning (self-study).

Sections 1, 2, 3 and 5 (Listening, Presentation, Controlled Practice, and Word Check) can be worked through with or without a teacher. Section 4 (Transfer) can be worked through by students in pairs or groups without a teacher, but some form of teacher monitoring is advisable.

Teacher's Notes

Uses of the material

1. As a complete course for students of Business English.
2. As supplementary material to a General English course for students with an interest in or a need for Business English.
3. As a self-study/homework component for a Business English course.
4. As follow-up material on completion of a Business English course.

Selection of material

The units are not graded. Teachers may, therefore, select according to:

1. Topic (see Contents page)
2. Language area/skill (see Contents page).

Using a unit

1. Listening

At the beginning of each unit there is a short introduction to the topic.
The input text for each unit is a listening passage.

   i Prepare the students for the task. Make sure they are absolutely sure what they have to do.
   ii Play the tape right through, without stopping.
   iii For many students it will be necessary to give them an opportunity to listen to the tape again. Replay the tape, stopping at appropriate places.
   iv Let the students check their answers with the Key.
   v Play the tape again if there are major differences between the Key and the students' answers.
   vi Refer the students to the Word Check (Section 5) if there are vocabulary problems.

2. Presentation

   i Ask the students to read through the presentation and explanation of the language area.
   ii Get them to give you additional examples of the language presented.
   iii If necessary, look at the tapescript in the Key to identify exponents of the language.

3. Controlled practice

   i Ask the students to complete the exercises and then check their answers with the Key.
   ii Advise on alternative answers or give more practice where necessary.

4. Transfer

These activities involve speaking — mostly pair work.

  i Divide the class into pairs.

  ii Assign roles (Student A and Student B). Make sure they only look at their own role/ information (Student B's information is always in the Key section).

  iii Monitor the pairs while they carry out the speaking transfer, prompting the use of practised language if necessary.

5. Word check

The words are taken from the listening passages. The glossary only provides definitions. This section can be used before, during or after the listening activity.

Note
The following symbols have been used to indicate what is missing in the exercises:

— — — — —   one or more words;
_____   only one word.

Notes to the Student

Who is it for?

This material is for students who have some previous knowledge of English and wish to apply it in a business context. It can be used by students working alone, as self-study or homework material during a business course, or as follow-up material after a business course.

Selection of material

You can work through the material starting at Unit 1. Alternatively, you can choose units on the basis of the topic or the language area or skill covered (see Contents page).

Using a unit

All of the units can be done without a teacher. All the sections in a unit can also be done without a teacher except for the Transfer activities (but see below).

1. Listening

This tells you something about the unit. All the listening activities have an exercise with them.

i Read through the introduction to the Listening section. Make sure you understand what you have to do while you are listening.
ii Play the tape right through without stopping.
iii As you listen, try to do the exercise.
iv If necessary listen to the tape again. Stop the tape and replay sections if you need to.
v Check your answers with the Key at the back of the book.
vi If your answers are wrong, listen again. You can check the tapescript in the Key. Use the Word Check if you cannot understand some of the words.

2. Presentation

i Read carefully through the presentation and explanation of the language area.
ii Try to remember how this language was used on the tape. If you wish, listen to the tape again.

3. Controlled practice

i Complete the exercises.
ii Check your answers with the Key.

iii If your answers are wrong, look again at the Presentation, and try to see why you have made mistakes.

4. Transfer

These activities involve speaking. You can do the pair work speaking activities without a teacher. However, these activities are best done with a teacher who can correct your spoken language.

If you do the pair work speaking activities with a colleague, follow this procedure:

i Decide who is Student A and who is Student B.
ii Student A should *only* look at the Student A copy.
iii Student B should *only* look at the Student B copy in the Key section.
iv Carry out the Transfer activity. Try to use the language you have learnt.

5. Word check

The words are taken from the listening passages. Try to think how you could use these words yourself.

Note
We have used the following symbols. They show you what is missing in the exercises:

＿ ＿ ＿ ＿ ＿   one or more words;
＿＿＿＿＿＿   only one word.

First meetings 1

(introductions and greetings)

---

1. Listening 🔘 ───────────────────────────

First you are going to listen to a number of people introducing themselves. Some of the introductions involve just two people; some involve three. As you listen, match up the names. The first one has been done for you.

1st person	*2nd person*	*3rd person*
Günther Klein	Mr Roberts	
Paul Matthews	John	Philip
Tom	Geoff Snowdon	Francis
Peter	Maxine	Dr Mannheim
Herr Tübingen	Francine	Roger
Jane	Akira Mishima	
Tony	Susan	

(Günther Klein is linked by a line to Geoff Snowdon.)

─────────────────────────────────── 🔘

---

2. Presentation

Introductions often include these steps:

greeting	or	request for introduction
introduction		introduction
response to greeting		response to greeting

You heard two types of introduction:

introducing yourself
introducing someone else

2.1 Introducing yourself

Greeting	*Introduction*		*Response*
Hello	Let me introduce myself.	My name's _____	Pleased to meet you. I'm _____
Good morning/ afternoon	My name's _____		Nice to meet you. Mine's _____
How do you do?	I'm _____		Nice to meet you. I'm _____

1

2.2 Introducing someone else

Request for introduction	*Introduction*	*Response*
_____, could you introduce me to _____?	Of course _____ Let me introduce you to _____	Nice to meet you.
_____, I haven't met _____	I'm sorry. _____, this is _____	Very nice to meet you.
_____, I don't know anyone here. You'll have to introduce me.	Of course, I'll introduce you to _____. _____, this is _____	Nice to meet you.
	Let me introduce you two. _____, this is _____	Nice to meet you.

Notes
1. Some introductions are more formal than others. The use of first names indicates *informality*.
2. In English-speaking cultures, people usually *shake hands* on first meeting.

Now listen again and indicate whether the introduction is *formal* (F) or *informal* (I). The first one has been done for you.

Introduction 1 (F)   Introduction 5 ( )
Introduction 2 ( )   Introduction 6 ( )
Introduction 3 ( )   Introduction 7 ( )
Introduction 4 ( )

3. Controlled practice

Complete the introductions:

1. Peter King introduces himself to Jack Simpson:
   PETER KING: Hello, _ _ _ _ _. My name's Peter King.
   JACK SIMPSON: _ _ _ _ _, I'm Jack Simpson.

2. Philip introduces Sarah to James:
   SARAH: Philip, I _ _ _ _ _ here. You'll have to _ _ _ _ _.
   PHILIP: Of _____, I'll _ _ _ _ _ to James. He's an old friend of mine. James,
   _ _ _ _ _ Sarah, she's just joined the company.
   JAMES: _ _ _ _ _, Sarah. Where do you come from?

3. Rod Burton introduces Pete Taylor to an important customer:
   PETE: Rod, I _ _ _ _ _ Mr Rogers, the Purchasing Manager from Kentons.
   ROD: I'm _____. Come and meet him. Mr Rogers, _ _ _ _ _ Pete
   Taylor, our Export Sales Manager.
   MR ROGERS: _ _ _ _ _. What countries do you cover?

4. Klaus Fischer introduces himself to an American visitor.
   KLAUS FISCHER: How _ _ _ _ _ _? My _ _ _ _ _ _.
   AMERICAN: _ _ _ _ _. _____ George Cole.

4. Transfer

GROUP WORK
Work in groups of three.

Introduce yourself to the others.
Introduce the other two to each other.
Ask to be introduced.

5. Word check

Marketing Manager − person in charge of the marketing department
Computer Manager − person in charge of the computer department
yet − up to now (in questions and negatives)
to be over − to be here on a visit from another country
host − person who invites or receives guests
to move − to go to live in a new house
these parts − this area

First meetings 2

(presenting yourself)

---

1. Listening

Manders PLC are having their annual party. Listen to the dialogues overheard at the party. Match up the people's names with their type of work. The first one has been done for you.

Names
1. Peter
2. John
3. Susan
4. Mike
5. Sarah
6. Mr Fields
7. Martin
8. Jean
9. Jean's husband

Type of work
a. Production
b. Personal Assistant
c. software development
d. market research
e. fashion design
f. Personnel
g. Accounts
h. Sales
i. Finance

---

2. Presentation

It is very common to present yourself in terms of your job. The job identifies the person. The dialogues that you heard follow a certain pattern:

Question/Comment	Filler	Response	Comment/Question
A: What do you do (for a living)?	B: Well	I'm in computers.	B: Not a bad job.
A: Do you work?	B:	Yes, I'm a fashion designer.	A: That's interesting.
A: What do you do (in the _____ Department)?	B: Oh	I'm on the market research side.	B: What about you? And you?
A: I haven't seen you around before.	B:	No, I've just started with Manders. I'm in the Sales Department.	A: What do you do there?

4

Notes

1. We often use the *simple present* when talking about jobs, e.g.
   A: What do you do?
   B: I work for Manders.
2. We use a variety of prepositions to indicate work relationships, e.g.
   I work for Manders (they are my employers)
   I work at Manders (the place)
   I work with Manders (a sense of collaboration)
   I'm in computers (general type of work)
   I'm on the market research side (general type of work)
   I'm in the Sales Department (specific place of work)
3. After the first question has been answered, a further comment or question may come from either A or B (see above).

3. Controlled practice

A   Complete the sentences with an appropriate preposition:

1. What do you do _____ a living?
2. I work _____ Manders.
3. I work _____ the Personnel Department.
4. I'm _____ the recruitment side.
5. I'm _____ fashion design.
6. He's _____ the Production Department.
7. I work _____ home.
8. She's been _____ Manders _____ years.

B   Choose the most appropriate response:

1. I'm in computers. What about you?
   (a) Oh, I live in London.
   (b) Well, I work in Sales.
   (c) Oh, I've been here for years.

2. I'm Mr Jones' secretary. He's the Production Manager.
   (a) Ah, that's interesting.
   (b) Is that one of your colleagues over there?
   (c) Oh, I haven't met him.

3. I live in Paris. What about you?
   (a) I'm a fashion designer.
   (b) Well, I come from the North.
   (c) I work from home.

4. My husband's in the Production Department.
   (a) I'm in the Sales Department.
   (b) Not a bad job.
   (c) Oh yes, I think I've met him.

5. Hello, I'm Sarah. I haven't seen you around before.
   (a) What do you do for a living?
   (b) Is that one of your colleagues?
   (c) No, I'm new here.

5

4. Transfer

PAIR WORK

Student B: Turn to the Key Section.

Student A: Use the business cards below to practise introductory conversations. Tell Student B about your job and place of work, and find out about Student B's occupation.

MANDERS INTERNATIONAL
Derek Malcolm, Sales Director

25 Salisbury Drive, London SW1

Tel: 01-456-6550   *Telex:* 75371

PETCON PETROLEUM CONSULTANCY AB
Leif Andersson, *Marketing Consultant*

45 Strangatan, Stavanger, Norway (office)
62 Solveigatan, Oslo, Norway (home)
Tel: 4-54788 (office)   1-634211 (home)

TELECON Spa.
Franco Brunello
Export Sales Manager

23 via Roma, Milano, Italy
Tel: 5-633421
Telex: TCON 766521

---

5. Word check

PLC − Public Limited Company. A company whose shares can be bought on the Stock Exchange

annual − every year

software − programs for a computer system

development − planning new products

Personnel Department − section of a company which deals with staff welfare, records, training and recruitment

colleague − fellow worker in a company or profession

Accounts Department − section of a company which deals with money paid or received

market research − examining the possible demand for a product before it is put on the market

Personal Assistant − secretary who provides special help to a manager or director

Finance − section of a company which controls a company's money

Production Department − section of a company which deals with the making of the company's products

fashion designer − person who plans new styles in clothes

6

UNIT 3 **First contact**

(social English 1)

___

1. Listening ⌷oo⌷ ────────────────────────

When you meet someone for the first time and start up a conversation, it is important to find points of common interest so that the conversation can run smoothly. Listen to the five dialogues on the tape. Decide if you think they are successful (√) or not (X) in making initial contact.

	Successful (√)	*Unsuccessful (X)*
Dialogue 1		
Dialogue 2		
Dialogue 3		
Dialogue 4		
Dialogue 5		

Now listen again and note down the answers to these questions.

Dialogue 1: Has the visitor been to Japan before? _____
Dialogue 2: Which hotel is the visitor staying in? _____
Dialogue 3: What topic of common interest do they find? _____
Dialogue 4: What topic of common interest do they find? _____
Dialogue 5: What topic of common interest do they find? _____

────────────────────────────────── ⌷oo⌷

2. Presentation

Successful conversation depends on finding a topic both people can easily talk about. One way of reaching this point is to follow a number of steps until a topic of common interest is found. A typical sequence might be:

Speaker	Step
A	opening question
B	immediate answer
A	follow-up question
B	immediate answer
B	additional comment
A	next question
A/B	topic of common interest

Now look more closely at the typical sequence of conversation.

2.1 Opening question

Is this your first trip to _____?
How was your trip?

2.2 Immediate answer

Yes, it is.
Fine, thanks.

2.3 Follow-up question

Are you staying long?
Business or pleasure?

2.4 Immediate answer

No.
Business.

Note
These answers are *not* helpful in finding a common interest. You need to make an additional comment.

2.5 Additional comment

But hopefully not my last.
Unfortunately only a couple of weeks.
Business, I'm afraid. My company is setting up an office here in Tokyo.

2.6 Next question

Have you found time to see much?
Really, where is your company based?

2.7 Establishing topic of common interest

Are you interested in gardens?
Oh, I visited Detroit a couple of years ago.
That's a coincidence. My wife is in fashion too.

3. Controlled practice

The following four dialogues are in the wrong order. Rearrange them to make a natural flow of conversation.

Dialogue 1
  — Really? What did you expect? ( )
  — No, I've been to the States before, but this is the first time in Atlanta. ( )
  — So, what do you think of Atlanta? ( )
  — Fine, I'll see what I can arrange. ( )
  — Well, it's not what I expected. ( )
  — There is a part like that. You must let me show you around. ( )
  — Well, I suppose I thought it would be more traditional. ( )
  — That would be interesting. ( )
  — Is this your first trip over here? (1)

Dialogue 2
— I'm sure. I hope to get back here again. ( )
— That's a pity. There's a lot to see. ( )
— Good. Are you here on business then? ( )
— Are you staying long? ( )
— Really? That's interesting. What line are you in? ( )
— No, just a couple of days. ( )
— Yes, we're thinking of setting up an office here. ( )

Dialogue 3
— That would be nice. ( )
— That's interesting. My son is an editor on the local paper. ( )
— I believe you're in journalism. ( )
— Really? I expect I'll meet him. ( )
— Yes, that's right — on the editorial side. ( )
— Yes, what about coming round for a drink? I could introduce you to him. ( )

Dialogue 4
— Scotland. This time of year it's pretty cold. ( )
— A bit warmer than back home. ( )
— Well, if you do come across, you must visit us. ( )
— Oh, so where do you come from? ( )
— Yes, that's right. The best time to visit is in the summer. ( )
— I can imagine. I've never been but people tell me it's very beautiful. ( )
— How do you find the weather here? ( )
— Maybe I'll get across next year. ( )

4. Transfer

PAIR WORK

Engage your partner in conversation. Try to establish a common interest — e.g. a place, a hobby, a job, family, etc.

5. Word check

trip — journey to a foreign country
interesting — something which takes and keeps one's interest, e.g. Tokyo is an interesting city
hopefully — I hope that . . .
interested — having or showing interest, e.g. are you interested in gardens?
hobby — free time activity
unfortunately — by bad luck
pleasure — enjoyment
to set up — to establish
to be based — to have one's headquarters
fashion — new styles in clothes
design — planning and drawing
fashion designer — person who plans new styles in clothes
coincidence — surprising combination of events, happening by chance
to fix ... up — to arrange

UNIT 4 **Further contact**

(social English 2)

---

1. Listening 🔘 ──────────────────────

Responding appropriately in social situations is an important part of communication. The following is an example of an appropriate response:

May I come in?   →   *Yes, of course.*

On the tape you will hear a number of responses. Decide whether the responses you hear are appropriate (√) or not (X). The first one has been done for you.

1. √	6.	11.
2.	7.	12.
3.	8.	13.
4.	9.	14.
5.	10.	15.

Now listen again. This time all the responses are appropriate.

── 🔘

---

2. Presentation

Polite responses can be grouped into several categories. This section tells you what to say in different situations.

2.1 When someone thanks you

Thanks for the help.   →   Not at all/You're welcome.
Thanks for the lovely meal.   →   Glad you liked/enjoyed it.

2.2 When someone apologises

Sorry, I must have got the wrong number.   →   It doesn't matter/Don't worry/Never
                                                                      mind.

2.3 When someone invites you

Would you like to come to dinner?   →   Yes, I'd like/love to.
How about a drink?   →   That would be nice/That's a good idea.

11

2.4 When someone asks your permission

2.4.1 If the answer is 'yes'
May I come in? → Yes, of course/Please do/Certainly.
Do you mind if I smoke? → No, of course not/No, not at all.

2.4.2 If the answer is 'no'
Do you mind if I smoke? → Well, actually I'd prefer you not to/I'd rather you didn't.

2.5 When someone asks you to pass something

Could you hand me that pen? → Of course. Here you are.

2.6 When someone has bad news

I didn't get that job. → Never mind. Better luck next time.
My father died last night. → Oh, I am sorry to hear that.

2.7 When someone has good news

We've had a fantastic year. → I'm glad to hear that/Congratulations.

2.8 When someone has surprising news

He's 99, you know! → Really?

2.9 When you agree with someone's opinion/share someone's hopes

I think we should leave now. → So do I.
I hope it stays dry. → I hope so too/Me too.

2.10 When you return someone's good wishes

Have a good weekend. → You too/Same to you.

3. Controlled practice

Write down an appropriate response. The first one has been done for you.
1. We lost the match. _Never mind. Better luck next time._ _ _ _ _ _ _
2. Do you mind if I open the window? _ _ _ _ _ _ _ _ _ _ _ _ _ _ _ _ _.
3. Would you like to go to a concert this evening? _ _ _ _ _ _ _ _ _ _ _ _ _ _
_ _ _ _ _ _ _ _ _ _.

4. Sorry, I interrupted you. __ __ __ __ __ __ __ __ __ __ __ __ __ __ __ __ __ __ __.

5. Could you pass me the file? __ __ __ __ __ __ __ __ __ __ __ __ __ __ __ __ __ __.

6. I hope he gets the job. __ __ __ __ __ __ __ __ __ __ __ __ __ __ __ __ __ __ __.

7. Have a good Christmas. __ __ __ __ __ __ __ __ __ __ __ __ __ __ __ __ __ __ __.

8. She's only 18 and she's already married with two children! __ __ __ __ __ __ __ __ __ __ __ __ __?

9. I think it's going to rain. __ __ __ __ __ __ __ __ __ __ __ __ __ __ __ __ __ __.

10. Thanks. That was a delicious meal. __ __ __ __ __ __ __ __ __ __ __ __ __ __ __ __.

11. My car broke down again this morning. __.

12. Can I see you for a moment? __ __ __ __ __ __ __ __ __ __ __ __ __ __ __ __ __ __.

13. How about something to eat? __ __ __ __ __ __ __ __ __ __ __ __ __ __ __ __ __ __.

14. You must come round for dinner. __ __ __ __ __ __ __ __ __ __ __ __ __ __ __ __ __.

15. I'm sorry. I've taken the wrong file. __ __ __ __ __ __ __ __ __ __ __ __ __ __ __ __.

4. Transfer

PAIR WORK

1. **Student B:** Turn to the Key Section.
   Student A: Go through the categories listed above with Student B — thank, apologise, invite, etc.

   Student B should respond appropriately.
2. When you have finished, Student B will make some statements. You should respond appropriately.

5. Word check

to respond — to reply
response — answer
appropriately — in the right way
lovely — enjoyable
glad — happy, pleased
to hand — to give
concert — musical performance

Company organisation

(presenting the company)

1. Listening 🎧

Listen to the presentation about Rossomon PLC. As you listen, complete the organisation chart below:

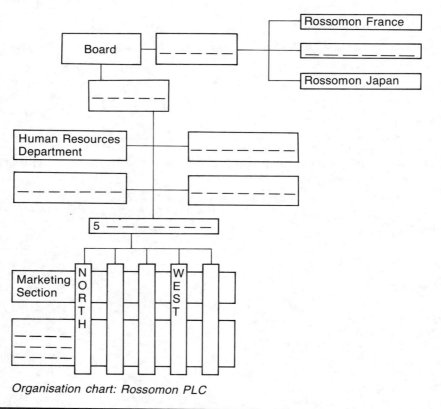

Organisation chart: Rossomon PLC

2. Presentation

Below is some of the language used to describe an organisation in terms of:

hierarchy
responsibilities/functions
titles
affiliates
structure

2.1 Hierarchy

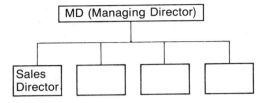

The company is *headed by* the MD.
The Sales Director *reports to* the MD.
The Sales Director *is under* the MD.
The Sales Director *is accountable to* the MD.

The Sales Director *is supported by* a Sales team.
The Sales Director *is assisted by* a Sales Assistant.

2.2 Responsibilities/functions

The Finance Department *is responsible for* accounting.
The R & D Department *takes care of* new product development.
The Administration Manager *is in charge of* personnel.

2.3 Titles

Below are the main managerial titles with the US equivalents in brackets:

Chairman (President)
Managing Director (Chief Executive Officer/Senior Vice-President)
Finance Director (Vice-President — Finance)
Sales Manager (Sales Director)

Note
The Directors and Chairman of a company usually sit on the Board of Directors (Executive Board).

2.4 Affiliates

X is the *parent company.*
A, B and C are *subsidiaries* (more than 50% owned by the parent).

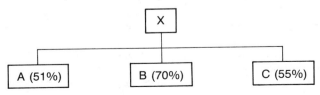

2.5 Structure

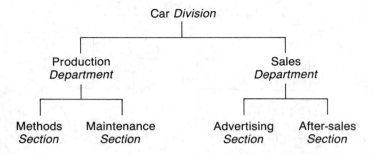

Car *Division*

Production *Department* — Sales *Department*

Methods *Section* — Maintenance *Section* — Advertising *Section* — After-sales *Section*

3. Controlled practice

Use the organisation chart in the Listening section and the language above to complete the sentences:

1. The Managing Director _ _ _ _ _ to the Board.
2. The Managing Director _ _ _ _ _ for running the company.
3. The Managing Director _ _ _ _ _ by four executive departments.
4. _____ the Managing Director, there are five regional divisions.
5. Each Regional Manager _ _ _ _ _ of a territory.
6. The five regions _ _ _ _ _ by two other sections — Marketing and Technical Services.
7. The Section Leaders _ _ _ _ _ the Regional Managers.
8. In addition to the _ _ _ _ _ _ company, Rossomon has three _ _ _ _ _: Rossomon France, Germany and Japan.
9. The subsidiaries _ _ _ _ _ to the Export Sales Department.
10. The Export Sales Department is _ _ _ _ _ to the Board.

4. Transfer
PAIR WORK
1. **Student B:** Turn to the Key Section.
   Student A: Describe the management structure of a typical British company to Student B. Use the organisation chart at the top of page 17.

2. Student B will now describe the managerial structure of a typical American company. Use the information you hear to complete the organisation chart opposite.

5. Word check

organisational — showing the way a company is organised
structure — organisation
Managing Director — director who is in charge of a whole company

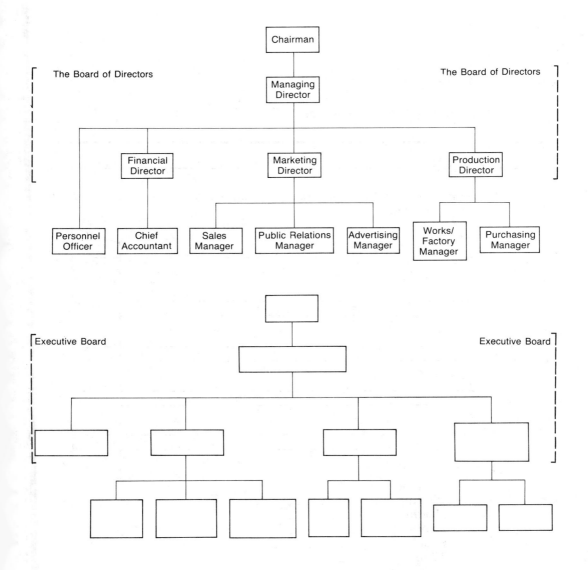

executives — people who put decisions into action
personnel — staff
training — teaching employees how to do something
rationalisation — making more efficient
region — part of a country
to split — to divide
matrix (basis) — organised according to two sets of criteria, e.g. geographical and functional
section — part of a company
subsidiary — company which is owned by a parent company
affiliate — company wholly or partly owned by another company

(describing product features)

1. Listening

Listen to the phone call about the supply of some office shelving systems. As you listen, fill in the missing information.

Dimensions:	Width	_ _ _ _ _ _
	Height	_ _ _ _ _ _
	Depth	_ _ _ _ _ _
Delivery:	Cost	_ _ _ _ _ _
	Time	_ _ _ _ _ _
Price:	Unit price	_ _ _ _ _ _
	Discount price	_ _ _ _ _ for 10 units
Guarantee period		_ _ _ _ _
Average life		_ _ _ _ _

2. Presentation

In the telephone conversation the speakers discussed:

dimensions
time
cost

Here is some of the language you heard.

2.1 Dimensions

Questions: How *wide* are they? (*note the adjective form*)
What's the *width*? (*note the noun form*)
How *high* are they?
What's the *height*?
Answers: They're 3.5 metres *wide* (*note the position of the adjective*).
The *width* is 3.5 metres.
They're 2 metres *high*.
The *height* is 2 metres.

2.2 Time

Question: How long does it *take* after ordering? (*note the verb*)
Answer: It *takes* 2 weeks.

2.3 Cost

Questions: How much is it?
How much does it cost?
How much do you charge?
Answers: It's £98.
It costs £98.
We charge £98.

3. Controlled practice

A. Complete the following table. Use a dictionary if necessary.

Noun form	adjective	opposite adjective
width	————	————
————	long	————
depth	————	————
————	————	low
distance	————	————
speed	————	————
reliability	————	————

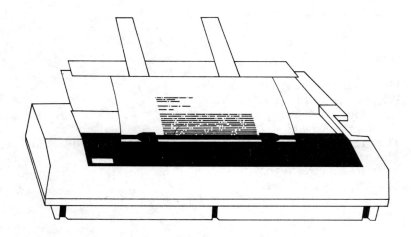

B. Ask questions about the technical and commercial specifications of the printer below. In all cases, use an *adjective* form or a *verb* form.

1. The width of the printer How wide is it _ _ _ _ _ _ _ _ _ _ _ _ _ _ _ _?

2. The depth of the printer _?

3. The speed of the printer _?

4. The time to deliver _?

5. The cost of delivery _?

6. The reliability of the printer _?

7. The length of the cable _?

8. The length of the guarantee period _ _ _ _ _ _ _ _ _ _ _ _ _ _ _ _ _ _ _?

9. The cost of the printer _?

10. The distance to the nearest service centre _?

4. Transfer

PAIR WORK

Student B: Turn to the Key Section.

Student A: Ask Student B for the following information about this typewriter:

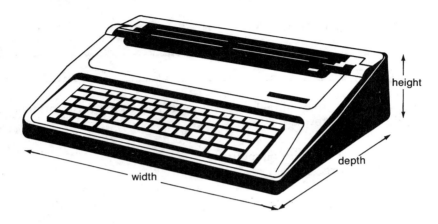

Dimensions: w: _ _ _ _ _ _
                                                         d: _ _ _ _ _ _
                                                         h: _ _ _ _ _ _

Delivery: time: _ _ _ _ _ _
                                                 cost: _ _ _ _ _ _

Price: for one: _ _ _ _ _ _
                       for more than five: _ _ _ _ _ _

Guarantee period: _ _ _ _ _

5. Word check

shelving – rows of shelves
to enquire – to ask
specifications – detailed information
flexible – movable
to fit – to fix, to attach
to stick out – to reach a position further than is wanted
delivery – transport of goods to a customer's address
to deliver – to transport goods to a customer's address
warehouse – large building where goods are stored
area – part of a town
charge – money which must be paid
to place an order – to order
to guarantee – to promise that something will work well
standard – normal
discount – percentage by which a seller reduces the full price for a buyer
to round ... off – to increase/decrease to the nearest full figure
sturdy – strong
average – normal

UNIT 7 **Travel information**

(requesting information)

---

1. Listening ⏏

Listen to the dialogues. In each dialogue, a traveller is asking for information. As you listen, note down the information.

Dialogue 1
Departure time of first plane to Hamburg: __ __ __ __ __
Arrival time at Hamburg: __ __ __ __ __

Dialogue 2
Departure point of airport bus: __ __ __ __ __

Dialogue 3
Platform number: __ __ __ __ __
Which end of station: __ __ __ __ __

Dialogue 4
Number of sleeping compartments on train: __ __ __ __ __
Location of dining car on train: __ __ __ __ __

⏏

2. Presentation

In the Listening section the traveller requested different types of information, using

WH-questions (where, when, how, etc.)
Yes/no questions

The traveller also used different language forms to request the information, i.e.

direct questions
polite questions

Now look at some of the language used for *requesting information*.

2.1 WH-questions

First we have WH-questions, divided into direct and polite questions.

2.1.1 Direct questions
When does the first plane for Hamburg leave?
Where does the airport bus leave from?

2.1.2 Polite questions
Could you tell me when the first plane for Hamburg leaves?
Do you happen to know where the airport bus leaves from?

Notes *Could you tell me* ...? is used when the person you are asking should know the answer (e.g. when he or she works in a travel information office).
Do you happen to know ...? is used when the person you are asking may not know the answer (e.g. when he or she is also a traveller).

2.2 Yes/no questions

Now we have Yes/no questions, divided into direct and polite questions.

2.2.1 Direct questions
Is there a dining car on this train?

2.2.2 Polite questions
Could you tell me whether/if there is a dining car on the train?

Notes 1. Notice that in both WH-questions and Yes/no questions, there is no inversion when you use the polite form.
e.g. Could you tell me if *there is* ...?
     Do you happen to know where the bus *leaves* ...?
2. Polite questions are generally used at the beginning of the conversation.

3. Controlled practice

A.   You are in a travel information office (and therefore expect the assistant to know the answers to your questions). Ask politely for the following information. The first one has been done for you.

1. The departure time of the first train to Rome.
   Could you tell me when the first train to Rome leaves?
2. The platform the train leaves from.
   _?
3. The arrival time in Rome.
   (When)
   _?
4. If there is a dining car.
   _?
5. If there are any sleeping compartments.
   _?

B.   You are visiting a town for the first time. You are lost and walk up to a person on the street who is looking at a map. You presume that he is also a stranger. Ask politely for the following information.

1. The name of this street.
   _?
2. If there is a tourist information office in the town.
   _?
3. The time the banks open.
   _?
4. The location of the underground car park.
   (Where) _?
5. The location of the nearest chemist.
   (Where) _?

C.   Ask directly for the following information.

1. If you have to change trains.
   _?
2. If platform five is the right platform for the train to Milan.
   _?
3. The departure time of the last train to Zurich.
   _?
4. The position in the train of the first class compartments.
   _?
5. The best route to the airport.
   _?

4. Transfer

PAIR WORK

1. **Student B:** Turn to the Key Section.
   Student A: You work as an information officer in a travel agency. Student B will ask you for information about planes from London to Paris. Use the information below to answer the questions.

```
From London Heathrow to Paris

Flight No.        Dep. time        Arr. time
BA 456            0830             1030
AF 678            0930             1130
BA 459            1000             1200
BA 454            1030             1230
AF 674            1130             1330
AF 673            1200             1400
BA 453            1430             1630
AF 679            1630             1830
BA 452            1700             1900
BA 451            1730             1930
AF 670            1900             2130
BA 450            2030             2230

NOTES:  1.  British Airways (BA) flights depart from Terminal 4
            Air France flights (AF) depart from Terminal 2
        2.  Check-in time on all flights: 30 mins before departure
```

2. **Student B:** Turn to the Key Section.
   Student A: You are walking along the street when a stranger (Student B) stops you and asks for information. Answer his/her questions using the information below.

   Transport from London to airport:
      underground — Piccadilly line
      airport bus — from Victoria station
   Journey time — you don't know

3. **Student B:** Turn to the Key Section.
   Student A: You want to travel from London to Paris by the Channel Tunnel. You go to the railway information office. Now ask Student B for the following information:

   the time of the first train to Paris
   the arrival time in Paris
   if it is necessary to reserve a seat
   the station the train leaves from
   the station the train arrives at

4. **Student B:** Turn to the Key Section.
   Student A: You are visiting London. You stop a stranger (Student B) in the street. Now ask Student B for the following information:

   the location of the nearest bus stop
   the time of the next bus to Victoria
   if you have to give the driver the exact fare

5. Word check

platform — place at a railway station where travellers get on and off a train
compartment — part of a train
dining car — carriage on a train where meals are served

UNIT 8 **Making arrangements**

(telephoning)

---

1. Listening 🔊

Listen to the three telephone calls. As you listen, complete the table below:

Call	Name of person called	Name of caller	Reason for call	Result of call
1	_ _ _ _ _	_ _ _ _ _	/ / / / /	_ _ _ _ _ _ _ _ _ _ _ _ _ _ _ _ _ _ _ _
2	_ _ _ _ _	_ _ _ _ _	_ _ _ _ _	_ _ _ _ _ _ _ _ _ _ _ _ _ _ _ _ _ _ _ _
3	_ _ _ _ _	_ _ _ _ _	_ _ _ _ _	_ _ _ _ _ _ _ _ _ _ _ _ _ _ _ _ _ _ _ _

🔊

2. Presentation

The telephone conversation you heard in the dialogues included a number of steps, in particular:

identifying yourself/your company
asking the caller to identify himself/herself
asking for connection
taking/leaving a message
explaining the reason for the call
making appointments
signing off

Now look at the language used for these steps.

2.1 Identifying yourself/your company

Krondike Electronics. Can I help you? (*a typical switchboard response*)
John Bird speaking.
This is Pete Edwards.
John here.

2.2 Asking the caller to identify himself/herself

Who's calling please?

2.3 Asking for a connection

I'd like to speak to _ _ _ _ _, please.
Could you put me through to _ _ _ _ _, please?
I'd like to speak to someone about deliveries, please.

2.4 Taking/leaving a message

I'm afraid he's out at the moment. Can I take a message?
Can you ask him to call me back?

2.5 Explaining the reason for the call

The reason I called is _ _ _ _ _.
I am (just) phoning to _ _ _ _ _.

2.6 Making appointments

Just a moment, I'll get my diary.
Could you manage Tuesday?
What about Friday?
Shall we say two o'clock?
I'm sorry, I'm out all day.
Friday would be fine.
That suits me.

2.7 Signing off

I look forward to seeing you.
Thanks for calling.
Goodbye.
Bye.

3. Controlled practice

A. Put the following extracts of telephone calls in the right order:

1. — Just a moment, Mr Jones, I'll put you through. ( )
    — Yes, I'd like to speak to Miss Rathbone. ( )
    — Peter Jones. ( )
    — Who's calling, please? ( )
    — Pan Electronics. Can I help you? ( )
2. — She's got it, but just in case, it's 01-253 4686. ( )
    — Yes, could you ask her to call me back? ( )
    — Mr Gottman here. Could I speak to Mrs Fields? ( )
    — Yes, of course. Could I have your number? ( )
    — I'm afraid she's out at the moment. Can I take a message? ( )
3. — I'm sorry, I'm out on Wednesday. ( )
    — Good, that suits me too. Shall we say 11 o'clock? ( )
    — Just a moment, I'll get my diary ... you said next week? ( )
    — Yes, could you manage Wednesday? ( )
    — What about Thursday then? ( )
    — Yes, Thursday morning would suit me fine. ( )

B. Choose the most appropriate response:

1. John Peterson speaking.   (a) Who's calling please?
                              (b) Peter Matthews here.
                              (c) Hello, John. This is Peter Matthews.
2. Can I take a message?   (a) I'd like to leave a message.
                              (b) Yes, could you ask him to call me back?
                              (c) Please tell him to give me a ring.
3. The reason I called is we're   (a) I don't believe it.
    having problems.   (b) Really? That surprises me.
                                   (c) I don't mind.
4. Could you manage Tuesday? (a) No, I can't.
                              (b) No.
                              (c) I'm afraid I can't.
5. So that's fixed — Friday at   (a) I'm afraid that's out of the question.
    11 o'clock.   (b) Right, I look forward to seeing you then.
                                  (c) Bye.

4. Transfer
PAIR WORK
This exercise consists of three telephone calls.

Student B: Turn to the Key Section.
Student A: 1. You are Mr/s Peterson. Telephone Student B. Ask to speak to Mr/s Rogers. You want to speak to him/her about an order. Your telephone number is (0732) 43550.
2. Mr/s Rogers calls you back. You want to order some shoes. Before you order you would like a price for 10 pairs (size 43). Confirm the price and tell him/her that you will put an order in the post.
3. You are Mr/s Taylor. Telephone Student B (Mr/s Dunn) to arrange a meeting to discuss your visit to Japan. You want to meet next week. Below is your diary for next week.

	Monday	Tuesday	Wednesday	Thursday	Friday
morning	Meeting with Sales Manager 10.00–12.00 Lunch with Ross		09.00 Meet sales reps 11.00 Drive to Manchester	Lunch with children	Leave for Japan BA 451 dep: 10.00
afternoon	Prepare report	Visit Ross factory 14.00–18.00	Visit two clients: 15.00 – Mr Peacock 16.00 – Miss Davis	Board Meeting 14.30–17.00	

5. Word check

installation – the process of putting new machines into an office or factory
complicated – difficult
technician – skilled technical worker
to sort out – to put right
to fix – to arrange
to manage – to be able to do something, e.g. meet on Tuesday
to suit – to be suitable or convenient

UNIT 9 **Information handling**

(checking and confirming)

1. Listening ▭

When telephoning it is very important to get certain facts right, for example the name, address, and telephone number. Listen to the following telephone call twice. The first time, listen to it from the point of view of the caller and complete his notes below. The second time, listen to it from the point of view of the person who answered and complete his notes.

First listening
Caller's Notes:

Name of Company: Priority Investments
Name of Corporate Finance Manager: __ __ __ __ __
Date of appointment: __ __ __ __ __
Time of appointment: __ __ __ __ __

Second listening
Called person's notes:

Caller's name: __ __ __ __ __
Caller's company: __ __ __ __ __
Caller's address: __ __ __ __ __
Tel. No.: __ __ __ __ __
Reason for call: __ __ __ __ __
Date of appointment: __ __ __ __ __
Time of appointment: __ __ __ __ __
Action: 1. Confirm appointment with Mr Foster.
        2. Send __ __ __ __ __

2. Presentation

In the telephone conversation the speakers followed a number of steps when handling and exchanging information, in particular:

clarifying information
asking for repetition
asking for spelling
showing understanding
correcting information
confirming information
acknowledging

Now look at the language used to handle information.

2.1 Clarifying information

Could you tell me exactly what _ _ _ _ _?

2.2 Asking for repetition

Could I have your name again please?
Could you repeat that?
I'm sorry I didn't catch that.

2.3 Asking for spelling

Could you spell that please?

2.4 Showing understanding

I see.
I've got that.
Right.

2.5 Correcting

No, not _Seanew_. _Seaview_
That's not right, it's _ _ _ _ _.

2.6 Confirming

Let me just repeat that, _ _ _ _ _.

2.7 Acknowledging

That's right.

Notes 1. Saying and repeating telephone numbers:

Look at the following number 01-455 2354. The number consists of three groups.
O is pronounced 'oh' or zero
455 is verbalised as four double five or four five five
The numbers should be grouped, e.g. 01 pause 455 pause 2354.

2. Spelling names:

A useful way to remember the pronunciation of some letters is to group them by vowel sound:

'ay'	'ee'	'e'	'y'	'oh'	'u'	'ar'
A	B	F	I	O	Q	R
H	C	L	Y		U	
J	D				W	
K	E					
	G					
	P					
	T					
	V					

3. Controlled practice

A.   Complete these short dialogues:

1. My name's Pinkerton.
   _____ _____ _____ _____ _____?
   Yes, it's P, I, N, K, E, R, T, O, N.
2. The address is 24 Tunnyside Lane.
   _____ _____ _____ _____?
   Yes, of course. 24 Tunnyside Lane.
3. My phone number is 0432-5686.
   0432-5688.
   _____, _____ 5686.
   _____ _____ _____ _____ _____ 0432-5686.
   _____ _____.
4. I'd like an appointment with Mr Dunn.
   _____ _____ _____ _____ _____ _____ you would like
   to discuss?
   Yes, I'd like to talk about extending my credit.
5. We would like to visit your factory with a view to buying it.
   _____ _____. When would you like to come?
6. The figure is 3.56 m.
   _____ _____ _____. And what was the other figure?
7. So an appointment at two would suit you. _____ _____ _____
   _____ _____ again, please?
   Yes, certainly, it's Macintosh.
   _____ _____ _____ _____ _____?
   Yes, M, A, C, I, N, T, O, S, H.

B.   Listen to the tape. You will hear some telephone numbers. After each number, there
will be a pause for you to repeat the number. You should write them down:

1. _____   4. _____
2. _____   5. _____
3. _____   6. _____

C.   Listen to the tape. You will hear some names and then a request to spell them. There
is a pause on the tape for you to spell them and then you will hear the correct spelling.
   The names are:

1. Peterson   5. Rifkind
2. Hardy   6. Thatcher
3. Glynis   7. Samuel
4. Matthews   8. Marjorie

4. Transfer

PAIR WORK

1. **Student B:** Turn to the Key Section.

   Student A: Telephone Student B. You are a supplier of sports equipment (ABC Sports). Before despatching an order to a new customer (Newsome Sports – Mr Savary), you want to check and confirm the following details:

   Name of company: Newsome Sports Ltd.
   Address: 25 Margate Hill, London NW10.
   Tel: _____ Telex: _____

   Order: 50 pairs of training shoes
   __ pairs of socks
   20 Greys Squash rackets
   Delivery date: 5.10.88
   Price: training shoes – £14.00 per pair
   socks – £3.00 per pair
   squash rackets – £22.00 per racket

2. **Student B:** Turn to the Key Section.

   Student A: You will receive a phone call from Student B. You are Mr/s Reynolds, Purchasing Department, Rossomon Skis. Student B works for Skiwear UK, who supply you with ski hats and gloves. He/she will want to check on the following order:

   Order No: 45688 Ski UK
   Order: 500 white ski hats
   450 leather ski gloves
   Delivery date: 6.11.88
   Price: ski hats: £1.50 per hat
   ski gloves: £2.00 per pair
   Payment terms: 60 days after delivery
   Delivery point: Rossomon Skis UK Ltd,
   45 Slough Road,
   Uxbridge.

5. Word check

corporate – referring to a whole company
appointment – arrangement to meet
to approach – to contact someone
investment – placing of money so that it will increase in value
convenient – suitable
to suit – to be suitable or convenient
current – present
prospectus – document which gives information to buyers or customers

Job routines

(present simple and expressions of frequency)

---

1. Listening 🔾

You will hear an interview between a journalist and a top businessman. The journalist is going to write an article called 'A day in the life of Paul Johnson'.

First look at the different activities in the table below. Then, as you listen, note the sequence of events in Paul Johnson's typical day. Some of them have been done for you.

Events	Sequence
Visit the plant	
Look at the post	
Have breakfast	
Meetings with Finance and Sales Directors	
Read a book	
Get up	1
Dinner engagement	
Leave for the office	
Go for a jog	
Lunch in the canteen	
Management/Board meetings	11
Read the newspapers	4
Meeting with deputy	
Finish work	
Go to sleep	

🔾

2. Presentation

There are two important features of the language used in the interview:

the present simple tense
expressions of frequency

2.1 The present simple tense

This is always used when we are talking about *characteristic/typical* actions:

He *gets up* at 5.
I *read* the newspapers after breakfast.

Note The 's' in the third person singular: he/she/it leaves.

We form questions in the present simple by using the auxiliary *do*:

When *do* you go to bed?
Does your wife work too?

Note The *does* form in the third person singular: *Does* he/she/it leave ...?

2.2 Expressions of frequency

These are divided into indefinite frequency and definite frequency.

The expressions of indefinite frequency have been given a relative numerical value in the list below, from 100% (always) to 0% (never). Of course, these numbers are only a general indication, not exact values.

Indefinite frequency	100% always
	90% usually
	75% often
	50% sometimes
	40% occasionally
	25% rarely/seldom
	10% hardly ever
	0% never
Definite frequency	every day *or:* daily
	every week weekly
	every month monthly
	every year yearly/annually
	once/twice/three times a day
	once/twice/three times a week
	etc.

Notes

1. Expressions of indefinite frequency are usually used with the present simple, e.g.

   I often go down to our plant . . .

2. Notice the position of the adverbs of indefinite frequency with the verb 'to be':

   I'm usually behind my desk by 7.30.

   and with other verbs:

   We usually have breakfast around 6.30. (*adverb before the verb*)
   Sometimes I have lunch out with customers or the bank manager. (*adverb at the beginning of the sentence*)

3. Controlled practice

A. Complete the dialogue with an appropriate question. The first one has been done for you.

A: *When do you get/wake up?*
B: Usually at six. At least my alarm clock goes off at six!
A: _ _ _ _ _ _ _ _ _ _ _ _ _ _ _ _ _ _?
B: No, I don't have breakfast straight away; first I go for a run.
A: _ _ _ _ _ _ _ _ _ _ _ _ _ _ _ _ _?
B: I sit down for breakfast about seven.
A: _ _ _ _ _ _ _ _ _ _ _ _ _ _ _ _ _?
B: After breakfast I read the papers.
A: _ _ _ _ _ _ _ _ _ _ _ _ _ _ _ _ _?
B: Oh, the Guardian and the Independent.
A: _ _ _ _ _ _ _ _ _ _ _ _ _ _ _ _ _?

B: I usually leave for the office about eight and I'm behind my desk by eight-thirty.

A: _ _ _ _ _ _ _ _ _ _ _ _ _ _ _?

B: I sort through the mail first.

A: _ _ _ _ _ _ _ _ _ _ _ _ _ _?

B: No, I don't have a secretary. I wish I had!

A: _ _ _ _ _ _ _ _ _ _ _ _ _ _?

B: No, I usually go out. Sometimes I even travel abroad.

A: _ _ _ _ _ _ _ _ _ _ _ _ _ _?

B: Oh, about four times a year. Usually to America.

B. Change the following sentences using an expression of indefinite frequency as indicated by the number in brackets.

e.g. I sort through my mail. (100%)
        I *always* sort through my mail.

1. I travel abroad. (40%)

_ _ _ _ _ _ _ _ _ _ _ _ _ _ _.

2. I have meetings. (75%)

_ _ _ _ _ _ _ _ _ _ _ _ _ _ _.

3. I see the Managing Director. (50%)

_ _ _ _ _ _ _ _ _ _ _ _ _ _ _.

4. I see the Chairman. (10%)

_ _ _ _ _ _ _ _ _ _ _ _ _ _ _.

5. I catch the seven o'clock bus. (100%)

_ _ _ _ _ _ _ _ _ _ _ _ _ _ _.

4. Transfer

PAIR WORK

Interview your partner. Find out about his/her daily routines.

5. Word check

interview — meeting to ask a person questions in order to collect information
journalist — person who writes for a newspaper
event — happening
jog — run
cover — front and back page of a newspaper
post — mail, letters
to sort out — to put in order
attention — action
deputy — person who takes the place of another
agenda — list of things to be done
up-to-date — informed of the latest information
canteen — factory restaurant
plant — factory
committee — official group of people who plan or organise for a larger group
board meeting — meeting of the directors of a company
engagement — appointment to do something, e.g. go out for dinner
midnight — 12 o'clock at night

UNIT 11 **Current projects**

(present continuous)

---

1. Listening

The Managing Director is getting up to date on the current projects of various departments. In some cases, they have no current projects, but have fixed plans for the future.
 As you listen, match the projects/plans with the departments. The first one has been done for you.

Projects/fixed plans

Plan advertising campaign

Test new prototype

Move to new offices

Do user study

Rationalise distribution network

Run quality training seminars

Look into new accounting system

Try to recruit new graduates

Install automated assembly line

Departments

EDP Department

Finance Department

Marketing Department

Production Department

Personnel Department

Administration Department

Research and Development Department

Transport Department

Management Services Department

---

2. Presentation

In this extract, the present continuous tense is used in two ways:

2.1. To indicate the present (and temporary) nature of the activity:

 We *are doing* a user study at the moment.
 We *are* currently *installing* the new automated assembly line.

 Note Time markers like: at the moment
                          currently
                          now

2.2. To indicate that a future plan is fixed (cannot be changed):

We *are moving* to new offices next week.
We *are running* a series of quality training seminars next month.

> *Note*   We use the present continuous to mean a present fixed plan to do something in the future.

3.   Controlled practice

Complete the tapescript of a meeting by inserting the right verb in the right form. Use each of the following verbs once:

to work on	to find
to run at	to come
to do	to happen
to approach	to plan
to teach	to think
to expand	to manage

MD: At the moment, the market _____ _____. So this is an opportunity we must take. Our advertising agency _____ _____ _____ a new campaign for next month. Now, what about Production?

PM: Currently we _____ _____ _____ 75% capacity — so, that gives us some spare capacity.

MD: Good, how _____ we _____ on staffing levels in the factory?

PM: We _____ _____ it difficult to recruit technicians. There seems to be a shortage on the job market.

MD: What _____ you _____ to do about it?

PM: Well, we _____ _____ of using a recruitment agency. A chap from a local agency _____ _____ in to see me on Monday to talk about it.

MD: Fine, what about cash flow? This upturn in the market is going to be a drain on cash.

FM: That's right. At the moment, we _____ _____ on an overdraft of about £50,000 and our current debts _____ _____ £85,000. I can go and talk to the Bank Manager about it. We've always been a good customer.

MD: Yes, do that as soon as possible. Finally, training. We're going to need some more sales reps and technicians in production. What _____ _____ at the moment in training?

TM: We _____ _____ a refresher sales course but we've got spare capacity . . .

4.   Transfer

GROUP WORK

Ask the other members of the group:

1. what current work they are involved in.
2. what fixed plans they have for the future.

5. Word check

up-to-date − informed of the latest information
current − present
project − plan
EDP − Electronic Data Processing
user − person who uses something
accounting − concerned with the work of recording money paid and received
to install − to put (a machine) into an office or factory
automated − worked automatically by machines
assembly line − production system where the product moves slowly through the factory
   with new sections added to it as it goes along
recruitment − looking for new staff
graduate − person who has a university or polytechnic degree
prototype − first model of a new machine before it goes into production
to rationalise − to make more efficient
distribution − way of sending goods
network − system which links different places, e.g. warehouses, together
cut − sudden lowering of costs
series − group

Business correspondence 1

(telexes)

---

1. Listening $\boxed{\text{oo}}$ ————————————————————

First look at the telexes below. Then listen to the three telephone calls. As you listen, match each telephone call to one of the telexes below:

Telex A: Telephone call _____

> RE: ORDER NO 6541
> WL DEL 25 TLCRCS + 2 MCRTSTS 14 JAN. RGRT DLY DEL.
> RGDS
> P REYNOLDS

Telex B: Telephone call _____

> RE: STUDY VST
> CFM ARRVL 6 AUG ENGRS FLT NO BA456 5 NOV 1430. THKS MTG THEM.
> RGDS
> TOM

Telex C: Telephone call _____

> FAO: MR PHILLIPS
> RE: ORD NO PT4351
> PLS INFM US ASAP WHEN ABOVE DEL EXPCTD.
> RGDS
> M JONES
> CONTRACT MGR

———————————————————————————— $\boxed{\text{oo}}$

2. Presentation

Telex language does not have fixed rules. Each writer has his/her own style. However, there are some common features of telexes.

2.1 Grammar

We generally miss out articles (the, a), pronouns, prepositions, and auxiliaries:

Full sentence: We have sent the spare parts to you.
Telex:　　　SENT SPARE PARTS

Future forms are not necessary if time is mentioned, and prepositions of time can be omitted:

Full sentence: The spare parts will arrive on 25 January.
Telex:　　　SPARE PARTS ARR 25 JAN

We generally use active sentences rather than passive:

Full sentence: The information was sent last week.
Telex:　　　SENT INFO LST WK

2.2 Reductions

We often miss out vowels (a, e, i, o, u), but not when they start the word:

Confirm　　　CFM
Obtain　　　OBTN

We usually use the beginning letters of longer words:

Information　　　INFO
Company　　　CO

We usually use the first three letters of months and days of the week:

January　　　JAN
Sunday　　　SUN

2.3 Expressions

Typical letter expressions are often abbreviated:

As soon as possible　　　ASAP
With best regards　　　RGDS
For the attention of　　　FAO

The **Telex Appendix** at the back of the book gives a list of commonly-used forms.

3. Controlled practice

A.　Understanding a telex
Read the following telex, then answer the questions.

3. Controlled practice

A.   Understanding a telex

Read the following telex, then answer the questions.

FAO: S JONES
RGRT MUST CHNG ARRVL TIME 14 NOV. NEW ARRVL TIME 1830 LHR. PLS ARRNG
PICK UP. PLS CHNG APPT MR TOMLINSON. SUGST 0930 15 NOV. NEW ITNRY
TUE 15 NOV LONDON WED 16 NOV EDINBURGH. DEP 1030 FRI
17 NOV. PLS CFM BY TLX APPT WITH TMLSON. SEE U MON.
RGDS
T BOWDEN

---

1. Who is the telex sent to?
2. Who is the telex from?
3. When will Mr Bowden be arriving at London Heathrow?
4. Will he take the underground from London Heathrow?
5. When does he want to meet Mr Tomlinson?
6. Will he be staying in London for the whole trip?
7. When will he be leaving?
8. What does he want S. Jones to confirm by telex?

B.   Writing telexes

Change the following sentences into telex language. The **Telex Appendix** at the back of the book will help you.

1. I would be grateful if you could confirm the receipt of my letter of 25 January.
   _.

2. We apologise sincerely for the late delivery of part numbers 754 and 431.
   _.

3. I will meet you on 28 February next week at the Plaza Hotel. Could you please bring some samples of your work?
   _.

4. Thank you very much for the documents you sent me last week. I will get a reply to you as soon as possible.
   _.

5. We would like to inform you that we have recently moved to new premises.
   _.

6. I look forward to seeing you on 26 January.
   Yours sincerely
   J. Biggins
   _.

4. Transfer
PAIR WORK

Student B: Turn to the Key Section.

Student A: You want to telex the Chamber of Commerce in Düsseldorf (details below). Write out a telex and give it to Student B. He/she will reply by telex.

Situation: Your contact person at the Chamber of Commerce is Mr/s Müller. You would like to know:

1. The names of Purchasing Managers in electronics firms in the Düsseldorf area.
2. Whether there is a trade fair for specialist electronics firms in Germany.

Remember to thank Mr/s Müller in advance.

5. Word check

contract − legal agreement between two people or organisations
to deliver − to transport goods to a customer
cement − grey powder, made from lime and clay, which becomes hard like stone after adding water and drying − used in building
contact − person to ask for help or advice
spare part − small piece of machinery used to replace part of a machine which is broken
form − official printed paper to be filled in with information
detail − piece of information
delivery − transport of goods to a customer's address
due − expected to arrive
to pick up − to collect
to confirm − to say that something is certain

(letter writing)

---

1. Listening 🔘

First read the letters below. Then listen to the three telephone calls. As you listen, match the telephone calls with the letters below.

Letter A: Telephone Call _____

Dear George

Just a note following our call. Sorry I couldn't lay my hands on the address. I've now found it:
Hotel Celeste
Sorrento
5120 Italy
Tel: (010) 3981 6582
See you soon and best wishes to the family

Geraldine

Geraldine

Letter B: Telephone Call _____

Subject: Financial Consultancy Contract

Dear Mr James

We would be grateful if you could send us a quotation for the above-mentioned contract. Details of the contract are attached.

Since the work is due to start in December, we would appreciate a reply at your earliest convenience.

Yours sincerely

J. Fish

J Fish
Corporate Finance Manager

Letter C: Telephone Call _____

Subject: Post of Office Manager

Dear Sir

Further to our telephone call this morning, I am writing to inform you of my availability for the above post.

I am now free to take up the post from 1 April this year.

I look forward to hearing from you.

Yours faithfully

Edward Bronson

Edward Bronson

_____ QO

2. Presentation

Business letters typically follow a number of steps, including the following:

opening and closing greetings
stating the reference at the beginning of the letter
requesting
explaining the reason for writing
thanking
enclosing documents
apologising
expressing urgency
confirming
ending the letter

Here is some of the language typical of business letters.

2.1 Opening and closing greetings

If you don't have a contact name:

Dear Sir or Madam

Yours faithfully

If you know the name of the person:

Dear Mr Jones
    Mrs
    Ms

Yours sincerely

If you know the person as a friend or close business colleague:

Dear James

Best wishes/regards

2.2 Stating the reference at the beginning of the letter

You can start with either

Subject: __ __ __ __ __

or an expression like:

With reference to __ __ __ __ __
I thank you for your letter of 1 July.
Further to our telephone conversation, __ __ __ __ __

2.3 Requesting

I would be grateful if you could __ __ __ __ __
I would appreciate it if you could __ __ __ __ __
Could you please __ __ __ __ __? (more informal)

2.4 Explaining the reason for writing

I am writing to inform/apply for/request/etc. __ __ __ __ __

2.5 Thanking

Thank you for __ __ __ __ __
We were very pleased to __ __ __ __ __

2.6 Enclosing documents

Where other documents are included with the letter, you can say:

Please find enclosed/attached __ __ __ __ __

2.7 Apologising

I regret that __ __ __ __ __
I am afraid that __ __ __ __ __

2.8 Expressing urgency

__ __ __ __ __ at your earliest convenience.
__ __ __ __ __ without delay.
__ __ __ __ __ as soon as possible.

2.9 Confirming

I am pleased to confirm that __ __ __ __ __
I confirm that __ __ __ __ __

3. Controlled practice

1. Select expressions from above according to the prompts given in brackets to complete this letter.

Dear Mr Phillips

_ _ _ _ _ (stating the reference) your letter of 10 August, _ _ _ _ _ (confirming) my participation at the International Sales Workshop in October.

_ _ _ _ _ (requesting) if you could send me details of the other participants and the programme. _ _ _ _ _ (enclosing documents) some suggestions for contributions.

_ _ _ _ _ (apologising) that I will not have the chance to see you before the workshop but _ _ _ _ _ (ending the letter) very much to meeting you in October.

Yours _ _ _ _ _ (closing greeting)

P. Denton

P Denton

2. Change the following telex into a letter. Refer to the *Telex Appendix* at the back of the book if you need help with the abbreviations.

FAO: THE FINANCE MANAGER
RE: FINANCIAL AUDIT
PLS CFM FLWG DTS OK — 21–23 JUN. RGRT MR HOWELL NOT AVB.
MR JENKINS WL DO AUDIT. HE WL CNTCT U DRCT RE ARRVL ETC. PLS FAX
DRAFT ACCTS ASAP.
RGDS
J SVENSSON
CHIEF AUDITOR

Some parts of the letter have already been done for you.

_ _ _ _ _: Financial Audit

Dear Sir

_ _ _ _ _ _ _ _ _ _ confirm that the dates of 21 to 23 June are convenient for the above-mentioned audit.

_ _ _ _ _ that Mr Howell will not be available; however, Mr Jenkins, one of our most experienced accountants, _ _ _ _ _ _ _ _ _ _. He will be in touch direct concerning _ _ _ _ _ and other details.

_ _ _ _ _ _ _ _ _ _ your draft accounts to us _ _ _ _ _.

J. Svensson

J Svensson
Chief Auditor

4. Transfer

Write a reply to the following letter.

TECHNOLOGY IN ENGINEERING CONFERENCE
45 Broughton Street, Brighton

J. Higgins
Purchasing Manager
Zacron Engineering
Unit 5
Hempstead Industrial Estate
Hemel Hempstead   25 May 1988

Dear Mr Higgins

We have pleasure in inviting you to our annual conference. This year it will be taking place at the Metropole Hotel, Brighton from 24 to 28 July.

We enclose details of the conference, accommodation arrangements and a provisional programme.

Last year you gave a very interesting presentation on the subject of 'Purchasing High Technology'. We would be very grateful if you would consider giving us an update on this.

We would appreciate it if you could confirm your participation at your earliest convenience.

Yours sincerely

P.Matthews

P Matthews
Conference Organiser

Your reply should include the following:

1. Reference to the above letter.
2. Confirmation of your participation.
3. Request for more information about the programme.
4. Apology for not being able to give another presentation (pressure of work — no time for preparation).
5. A polite phrase to end the letter.

Some parts of the letter have already been done for you.

Zacron Engineering
Unit 5
Hempstead Industrial Estate
Hemel Hempstead

Mr P Matthews
Technology in Engineering Conference
45 Broughton Street
Brighton

1 June 1988

Dear Mr Matthews

With reference to your letter of 25 May, I am pleased to _ _ _ _ _ _ _ _ _ _ _ _
_ _.

I would be grateful _
_ _ _ _ _.

Unfortunately, _
_ _ _ _ _ _ _ _ _ _. I am afraid _ _ _ _ _ _ _ _ _ _ _ _ _ _ _ _
_ _ _ _ _ _ _ _ _ _ _ _.

_ _.

Yours sincerely

J. Higgins

J. Higgins
Purchasing Manager

5. Word check

Letters
to lay one's hands on − to find
consultancy − act of giving specialist advice
contract − legal agreement between two parties
quotation − estimate of how much something will cost
above-mentioned − something written above or before in a letter
to attach − to fasten, to link
due − expected, supposed
to appreciate − to be thankful or grateful
post − job
availability − state of being able to take up a new job

Phone calls
to reply − to answer
urgently − immediately
to get back to − to phone again
to advertise − to announce publicly that a job is vacant
application − asking for something, e.g. a job, usually in writing
to recommend − to suggest
to drop a line − to write a short letter

UNIT 14 Out and about

(giving and understanding directions)

1. Listening 🔘

Listen to the four dialogues in which a visitor asks for directions to four places. After you have listened to each dialogue, indicate the number of the dialogue (1, 2, 3, or 4) describing the route to the destination.

Destination	Dialogue
a. The Minster	_____
b. St Sampson's Square	_____
c. The Post Office	_____
d. Viking Centre	_____

All directions start from the Railway Station (A2).

2. Presentation

Here is some of the language used for giving and understanding directions.

2.1 Asking the way

Could you tell me how to get to _ _ _ _ _?
the way to _ _ _ _ _?

2.2 Giving directions

Turn left/right.
Go straight ahead.
Walk over/under _ _ _ _ _ (bridges).
Go down _ _ _ _ _ (a street).

2.3 Landmarks

_ _ _ _ _ until you get to the junction _ _ _ _ _.
You'll see the castle on your right/left.
in front of you.
You'll come to _ _ _ _ _.
At the traffic lights, _ _ _ _ _.
When you reach _ _ _ _ _, _ _ _ _ _.

51

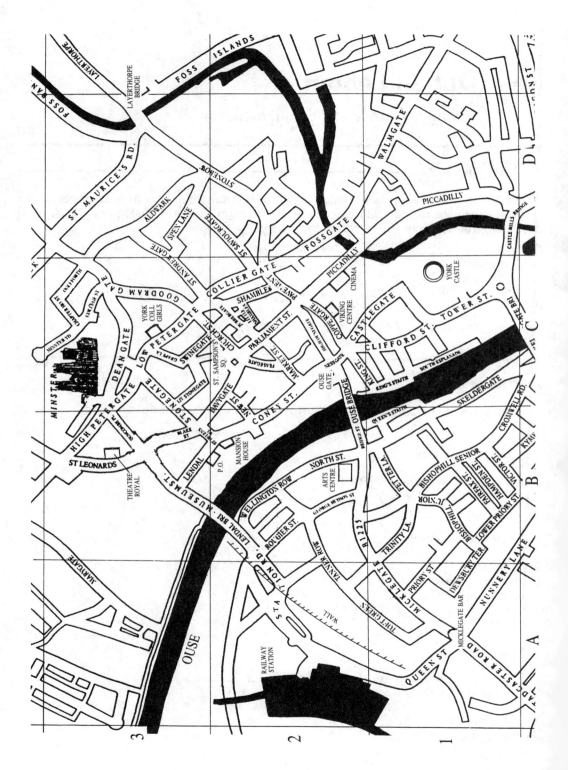

2.4 Showing understanding

Right.
I've got that.

2.5 Asking for repetition

Could you go over that last part again, please?
Sorry, I didn't get/catch that.

2.6 Checking understanding

Have you got that?
Is that clear?

3. Controlled practice

Use the map and the language above to complete these dialogues.

1. The way from the Minster (C3) to the cinema on Piccadilly (C2).
A: _ _ _ _ _ _ from the Minster to the cinema?
B: Yes, of course. _ _ _ _ _ _ Petergate into Low Petergate. _ _ _ _ _ _ the York
   College for Girls on your _ _ _ _ _ _.
A: York College for Girls on the left. I _ _ _ _ _ _.
B: Good. Continue down Low Petergate _ _ _ _ _ to the junction with Goodramgate.
   _ _ _ _ _?
A: Yes.
B: At the junction, go _ _ _ _ _ _ and then down Colliergate. _ _ _ _ _ _ the
   junction with Pavement, turn _ _ _ _ _ _ along Pavement.
A: _ _ _ _ _ _?
B: Yes, walk down Colliergate and then right along Pavement.
A: I _ _ _ _ _ _.
B: Then _ _ _ _ _ _ a junction with Parliament Street and Piccadilly. _ _ _ _ _ _
   along Piccadilly and _ _ _ _ _ _ the cinema _ _ _ _ _ _ right.
A: Cinema on the right. OK, I think I _ _ _ _ _ _. Thanks very much.
B: You're welcome.

2. The way from York Castle (C1) to The Arts Centre (B2).
A: Could you tell me how _ _ _ _ _ _?
B: Yes. _ _ _ _ _ _ Clifford Street _ _ _ _ _ _ Nessgate.
A: Right. Down Clifford Street into Nessgate.
B: That's it. _ _ _ _ _ _ with Ousegate, _ _ _ _ _ _ down Ousegate and then
   _ _ _ _ _ _ the Ouse Bridge.
A: I'm sorry, _ _ _ _ _ _.
B: Turn left and then walk over Ouse Bridge.
A: I _ _ _ _ _ _.
B: Good. _ _ _ _ _ _ the bridge take _ _ _ _ _ _ and _ _ _ _ _ _ the Arts Centre
   _ _ _ _ _ _.
A: First right after the bridge and the Centre is _ _ _ _ _ _.
B: That's right. Bye.
A: Thanks, bye.

4. Transfer

PAIR WORK

1. **Student B:** Turn to the Key Section.

   Student A: You are visiting York, and don't know the city at all. You are now standing on Layerthorpe Bridge (D3). You have an appointment at the Mansion House in St Helen's Square, but you don't know how to get there. You stop a stranger in the street (Student B) to ask for directions.

   Remember to repeat and check your understanding of the directions.

2. **Student A:** Now give Student B directions from Micklegate Bar (A1) to the Theatre Royal (B3).

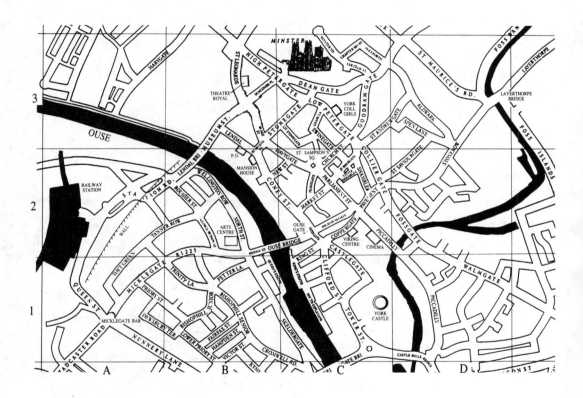

5. Word check

to get to – to reach
simple – easy
to get – to understand
clear – understood
traffic lights – coloured lights used for controlling and directing traffic
to go over – to repeat
pleasure – polite reply said in response to 'Thank you'
junction – place where two or more roads meet
you're welcome – polite reply said in response to 'Thank you'

UNIT 15 **Sales review**

(describing graphs)

---

1. Listening 🔘

Listen to the sales review. As you listen, match the product to the graph.

Products: AMAT, BMAT, CMAT

Graph 1
Sales performance: product _____

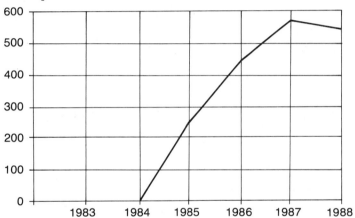

Graph 2
Sales performance: product _____

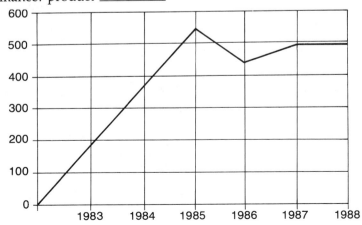

Graph 3
Sales performance: product _____

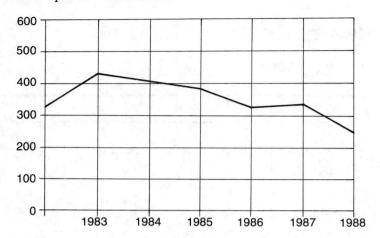

2. Presentation

In the Listening section you heard a presentation which included:
graph description
past tenses

Now look at the language that the presenter used.

2.1 Describing graphs

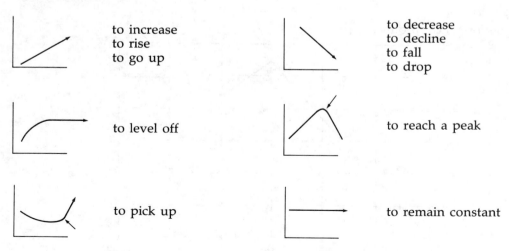

to increase
to rise
to go up

to decrease
to decline
to fall
to drop

to level off

to reach a peak

to pick up

to remain constant

2.2 The past tense

Use:

The past tense is used throughout the extract because the time is *finished* and marked by expressions like:

10 years ago
in 1987
by the end of 1987
last year

Form:

Regular verbs: end in 'ed' —	to reach → reached
	to remain → remained
	to increase → increased
	to drop → dropped
	to level → levelled
Irregular verbs:	to rise → rose
	to fall → fell
	to go → went
	to be → was/were

3. Controlled practice

Use the three graphs in Section 1 and the language above to complete the following sentences:

1. AMAT sales *reached* _____ _____ in 1983.
2. In 1984 and 1985 the sales _____ _____ at 400,000.
3. In 1987 sales f_____ to 330,000.
4. In 1988 the figure _____ 250,000.
5. From 1983 to 1985, BMAT sales r_____ steadily to a _____ of 550,000.
6. In 1986, sales d_____ badly to 450,000.
7. In 1987, sales _____ _____ to settle at this figure.
8. In 1988, they _____ _____ at this figure.
9. CMAT sales _____ _____ rapidly in 1984 to _____ 250,000.
10. In 1986, they _____ 450,000.
11. In 1987, sales i_____ to 580,000.
12. In 1988, they d_____ to 550,000.

4. Transfer
PAIR WORK
1. **Student B:** Turn to the Key Section.
   Student A: The graph below shows the performance of a product (sales and prices) between 1983 and 1987. Describe it to Student B.

Sales and prices

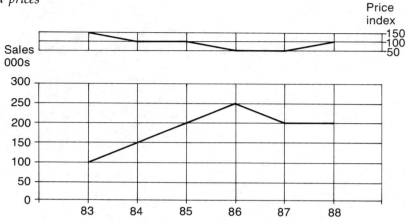

2. **Student A:** Now listen to Student B's description of the performance of a product (turnover and profits). As you listen complete the graph below.

Turnover and profits

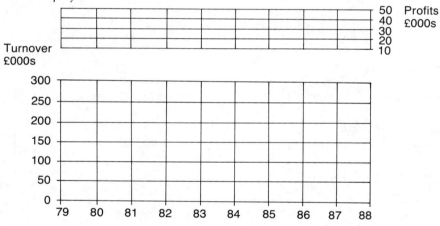

5. Word check

target — level, e.g. of sales, to aim for
performance — how good or bad the results are
product — thing which is made or manufactured
to launch — to put a new product on the market
peak — highest point
unit — single product
steadily — in a regular or continuous way
to settle — to stay at the same level
rapidly — quickly
slightly — not very much, a little
results — outcome of the year's trading

Sales forecasts

(intentions and predictions)

---

1. Listening 🔘

A Sales Director presents the sales targets for four products. As you listen, match the graphs with the products: AMAT, BMAT, CMAT and DMAT.

Graph 1
Product: _____

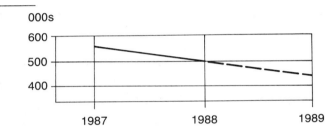

Graph 2
Product: _____

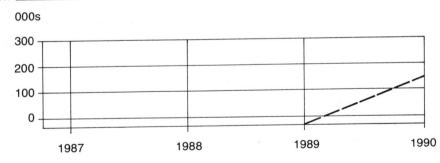

Graph 3
Product: _____

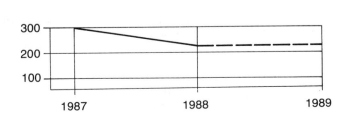

Graph 4
Product: _____

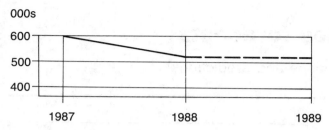

000s

600 —
500 —
400 —

1987   1988   1989

2. Presentation

When we talk about the future, we can do so either personally or impersonally. We can also indicate the degree of probability in terms of:

certainty
probability
possibility

Now look at the language used in the Listening section.

Personal form	*Impersonal form*	*Likelihood*
We are sure sales will _ _ _ _ _ _	Sales will (certainly) rise	Certainty
We intend to _ _ _ _ _ _	Sales are going to rise	
We expect sales will _ _ _ _ _ _	Sales should rise	Probability
We think sales will _ _ _ _ _ _	Sales will probably rise	
We hope sales will _ _ _ _ _ _	Sales may rise	Possibility
	Sales could rise	

3. Controlled practice

Use the table above to change these sentences into an equivalent personal or impersonal form. The first one has been done for you.

1. BMAT sales will probably reach their target.
   We expect/think BMAT sales will reach their target. (personal form)
2. I hope AMAT sales will be above target.
   _. (impersonal form)
3. We intend to launch the DMAT next year.
   _. (impersonal form)
4. I am sure CMAT sales will reach their target.
   _. (impersonal form)
5. The DMAT should replace the AMAT.
   _. (personal form)
6. We hope our German subsidiary will launch a new medium-range product in 1991.
   _. (impersonal form)

7. The Sales team intend to carry out a large-scale promotion campaign.
_ _. (impersonal form)
8. Total sales could be around £1,250,000 next year.
_ _. (personal form)
9. I think the campaign will be successful.
_ _. (impersonal form)
10. The R & D department hope to have the product ready by 1990.
_ _. (impersonal form)

4. Transfer

PAIR WORK

Student B: Turn to the Key Section.

Student A: You are a customer. Phone your supplier (Student B) and find out about the delivery dates of the following products. Note down the degree of likelihood of the supplier keeping to these dates.

Products	Delivery dates	Likelihood
office desks	_ _ _ _ _	_ _ _ _ _
office chairs	_ _ _ _ _	_ _ _ _ _
calendars	_ _ _ _ _	_ _ _ _ _
year planners	_ _ _ _ _	_ _ _ _ _
filing cabinets	_ _ _ _ _	_ _ _ _ _
security cupboards	_ _ _ _ _	_ _ _ _ _

Note

Ask questions like: When can we expect delivery _ _ _ _ _?
When do you think _ _ _ _ _?
etc.

When you have finished, compare your notes with Student B's information.

5. Word check

target — level to aim for
medium-term — referring to a period of about five years
roughly — about, approximately
pessimistic — feeling sure that things will work out badly
large-scale — working in a large way
promotion — advertising, publicity
campaign — business plan
to achieve — to succeed in doing something
optimistic — feeling sure that things will work out well
to balance out — to be equal
conservative — careful, not overestimating
forecast — calculation of future sales
to launch — to put a new product on the market
to take off — to start to rise quickly, to be a success (new product)
initially — at first
to complement — to go well with something else
eventually — finally
medium-range — of middle price or size, suitable for the middle of the market

UNIT 17 Company results

(present perfect v. past simple)

1. Listening 🔲

Listen to a company chairman making an end-of-year presentation. As you listen, complete his presentation notes.

Three areas:

1. Financial   a. Results   — turnover: + 14%
             — costs: _ _ _ _ _ _
             — _ _ _ _ _ _: +_ _ _ _ _ _
        b. Exports: _ _ _ _ _ _ _ _ _ _ _
          Domestic consumer market:
          _ _ _ _ _ _ _ _ _ _

2. _ _ _ _ _ _   a. Personnel Development
        b. Recruitment: _ _ _ _ _ _ _ _ _ _ _
        c. _ _ _ _ _ _: has expanded
          New areas: _ _ _ _ _ _ and _ _ _ _ _ _

3. _ _ _ _ _ _   a. The Research Dept has tested prototype engine
        b. _ _ _ _ _ _ _ _ _ _ _

🔲

2. Presentation

In his presentation, the chairman used the *present perfect* tense (has/have + past participle):

The results *have been* very pleasing.
The company *has performed* well.

He uses this tense because:

1. He is probably talking at the end of December — the year is not quite finished.
2. He doesn't specifically refer to time periods. Contrast the present perfect and the past simple in the following sentences:

   The company *has performed* well. (present perfect)
   The company *performed* well at the beginning of the year. (past simple)

3. Many of the events have a present impact, e.g.

   We *have invested* heavily in the European Technology Programme.

So, we can contrast the present perfect with the past simple, as follows:

1. We have done well this year. (*Time unfinished*)
   We did well last year. (*Time finished*)
2. I've been to Paris. (*Time not stated*)
   I went to Paris last week. (*Time stated*)
3. Our Research Department has thoroughly tested a new prototype. (*Present and future impact*)
   Our Research Department thoroughly tested a new prototype and found it was not effective. (*No present impact*)

3. Controlled practice

Put the verbs in brackets into an appropriate tense — present perfect or past simple.

1. Turnover _ _ _ _ _ _ by 14% last year. (*increase*)
2. The company _ _ _ _ _ _ disappointing results recently. (*have*)
3. The domestic consumer market _ _ _ _ _ _ very competitive. (*be*)
4. Two years ago we _ _ _ _ _ _ an updated product. (*launch*)
5. We _ _ _ _ _ _ 20 junior managers. (*recruit*)
6. _ _ _ _ _ _ you ever _ _ _ _ _ _ Australia? (*visit*)
7. We _ _ _ _ _ _ there last June. (*go*)
8. We _ _ _ _ _ _ not _ _ _ _ _ _ the results of the tests yet. (*receive*)
9. _ _ _ _ _ _ you _ _ _ _ _ _ the report? (*see*)
   Yes, it was interesting.
10. Three senior managers _ _ _ _ _ _ this year. (*retire*)

4. Transfer

PAIR WORK
Student B: Turn to the Key Section.
Student A: Find out whether Student B has or hasn't done the things in the list below. If the answer is yes, ask for further information about when/where/why he/she did them.

All the introductory questions should be in the present perfect. All the questions for further information (when/where/why etc.) should be in the past simple, e.g.

Have you (ever) travelled by hovercraft?
Where did you go to?
Why did you go there?
When was that?

1. Work abroad
2. Visit America
3. Chair a meeting
4. Make a presentation in English
5. Speak on the telephone in English
6. Fly on Concorde
7. Sleep in a tent
8. Drive a car on the left-hand side of the road.

5. Word check

chairman — person who is in charge of a meeting
review — general examination
results — outcome of the year's trading
turnover — amount of sales
to drop — to fall
profits — money gained which is more than money spent
domestic — home
competitive — hard, as a result of the activities of other companies in the same area
disappointing — below expectation
policy — decisions on the way of doing something
actually — in fact
to recruit — to get new staff
to expand — to get bigger
quality assurance — checking that the quality of a product is good
growth — increase in size
prototype — first model of a new machine before it goes into production

Company strategy

(conditional 1)

1. Listening ⊙⊙

Listen to the discussion about company strategy. Match the conditions to the results.
The first one has been done for you.

Conditions

1. Reduce prices
2. Margins smaller
3. Increase production
4. Invest in new plant
5. Upgrade product
6. Higher prices
7. Reduce manufacturing costs
8. Sub-contract production

Results

a. Cut unit costs
b. Job losses
c. Reduced sales
d. Market share increases
e. Cut profits
f. Unit costs come down
g. Higher profits
h. Adapt to market

2. Presentation

In this extract from a meeting, *conditional* sentences were used to express *possible* results.
The construction used was:

Condition
If we reduce prices
If we can reduce unit costs

Result
our market share will increase
that must put us in a strong position

Note
The present simple is used in the *condition*.
The future with 'will' or a modal in the present is used in the *result*.

We often reverse the sentence:

Result
But it'll mean job losses
Unit costs can only come down

Condition
if we sub-contract production
if we invest in new plant

3. Controlled practice

Make conditional sentences from the prompts below. You must decide which is the condition and which is the result, and use an appropriate verb, where necessary.

e.g. Sales increase/good advertising campaign
Sales will increase if we have a good advertising campaign
if there is a good advertising campaign

1. More satisfied customers/improve the delivery service
   _.
2. Rationalise production/unit costs reduced
   _.
3. Job losses/rationalise production
   _.
4. Install robots/lower labour costs
   _.
5. Price war/competitors enter the market
   _.
6. Charge higher prices/upgrade the product
   _.
7. Earn larger profits/increase our margins
   _.
8. No research/no new products
   _.
9. Not offer better salaries/not attract the best people
   _.
10. Fewer meetings/more time to do the job
    _.

4. Transfer

PAIR WORK
Student B: Turn to the Key Section.
Student A: Ask Student B 'What will happen if ...?

Conditions:
1. Your company moves to a new location?
2. Your English improves a lot?
3. You are offered a new job abroad?
4. You win the lottery?

5. Word check

strategy — plan of future action
to define — to find
flexible — which can be changed
objective — something which you aim for
market share — percentage of a total market which the sales of a company or product cover
to reduce — to make less or smaller

margins — difference between the buying and selling price
long-term — for a long period of time
prospect — possibility for the future
to invest — to spend money usefully
plant — factory
manufacturing — production
to upgrade — to make better
competitive — hard, as a result of the activities of other companies working in the same area
rapidly — quickly
to adapt — to change
to sub-contract — to agree with another company that they will do part of the work

UNIT 19 **Competition**

(comparison of adjectives)

---

1. Listening $\boxed{\infty}$

The Sales Manager of Brotherton PLC is talking about the company's main competitors. As you listen, complete the table below.

Rank in order 1–4:

	Age in market 1 = oldest	Market share 1 = biggest	Product price 1 = cheapest	Profitability 1 = most profitable
Brotherton				
Benton		1		
Zecron				
Mansell	1			

$\boxed{\text{O.O}}$

2. Presentation

In this extract you heard a variety of comparative and superlative forms of adjectives.

2.1 Adjectives with one syllable

long	long*er*	the long*est*
big	big*ger*	the big*gest*
low	low*er*	the low*est*
high	high*er*	the high*est*
late	lat*er*	the lat*est*

2.2 Two-syllable adjectives ending in 'y'

heavy	heav*ier*	the heav*iest*
early	earl*ier*	the earl*iest*

2.3 Adjectives with two or more syllables

reliable	*more* reliable	the *most* reliable
expensive	*more* expensive	the *most* expensive
profitable	*more* profitable	the *most* profitable

2.4 We can also modify the strength of the comparative adjective.

If we want to make it stronger, we can use *much*, e.g.

a much smaller market share
much more reliable

If we want to make it weaker, we can use *slightly*, e.g.

slightly higher prices
slightly longer

3. Controlled practice

Use the table in Section 1 and the language above to complete these sentences.

1. Mansell have been in the market _____ _____.
2. Brotherton entered the market _____ than Benton.
3. Benton entered the market ten years _____ than Brotherton.
4. Benton have _____ _____ market share.

5. Mansell have a much _____ market share than Brotherton.
6. Benton's products are sold at _____ _____ prices.
7. Mansell's products are sold at _____ _____ prices than Brotherton's.
8. Zecron's products are _____ _____ _____ than Brotherton's.
9. Mansell is _____ _____ profitable company.
10. Brotherton is _____ _____ than Benton.

4. Transfer

PAIR WORK

Student B: Turn to the Key Section.

Student A: Ask Student B questions so that you can complete the table below by inserting ranking figures (1−4). Ask questions like:

Which is the most _____ company?

Is _____ more _____ than _____?

Company	Turnover	Profitability	Share capital	Employees
Cittabank				
RA Chemicals				
Elton Oil				
Natelecom				

5. Word check

competition − trying to do better than another company
competitor − person or company who tries to do better than another person or company
competitive − hard, as a result of competition
to enter the market − to start to do business
to grow − to become bigger
rapidly − quickly
market share − percentage of a total market which the sales of a company cover
attractive(ly) − in a pleasant way
weakness − position of not being strong or active
major − important
return − official report of income and profits
investment − money spent usefully
plant − factory
to overtake − to pass
to achieve − to succeed in doing something
turnover − amount of sales
reliable − which can be trusted
(also **reliability**)
reputation − general opinion about something or someone
to hold on to − to keep

UNIT 20 **Stock control**

(countable and uncountable nouns)

1. Listening ⌒⊙

Two warehouse employees are doing a stock check. As you listen, complete the table below.

Item	too much	too little	too many	too few
liquid gas				
coal				
cable				
pipes				
boxes				
paper				
pallets				

⌒⊙

2. Presentation

English grammar divides nouns into *countable* and *uncountable*.

A *countable noun* has a singular and a plural form.
An *uncountable noun* has only a singular form.

Here are some examples:

Countable nouns
barrel — barrels
cannister — cannisters
ton — tons
letter — letters
computer — computers
machine — machines

Uncountable nouns
oil (and other liquids)
gas (and other gases)
wood (and other solids)
information
equipment
machinery
courage ⎫
honesty ⎬ *abstract nouns*
kindness ⎭

71

With countable nouns we use *many/few*, e.g.
How many computers do you have? Only *a few*.

With uncountable nouns we use *much/little*, e.g.
How much information do you need? Only *a little*.

3. Controlled practice

A   Classify the following nouns as *countable* (C) or *uncountable* (U).

table	diary
office	equipment
furniture	ink
telephone	wisdom
information	personnel
screen	person
advice	wife
data	safety
news	newspaper
service	paper
sale	security

B Complete the following sentences with much, many, little or few:

1. How _____ time have you got?
2. I'm sorry, I've only got a _____ money on me.
3. I can't give you _____ advice, I'm afraid.
4. I'll ring you back in a _____ minutes.
5. How _____ times have you been here?
6. I've only got a _____ coins, no notes.
7. There isn't _____ news today.
8. We shouldn't use so _____ paper now the computer is installed.
9. I like rooms with just a _____ furniture.
10. We've far too _____ items in stock.

4. Transfer

PAIR WORK

Student B: Turn to the Key Section.
Student A: You run a restaurant. Ask Student B what the stock situation is for the items in the list below. Ask questions like: How much/many __ __ __ __ __ have we got?

Items

flour	red house wine	spaghetti
sugar	white house wine	beef
salt	perrier water	salami
pepper	orange juice	cans of tomatoes
tomatoes	cans of beer	fruit
lettuces	bottles of coke	strawberries

5. Word check

stock control − making sure that enough stock is kept
warehouse − large building where goods are stored
employee − person who works for a company
stock check − looking at stock to see if there is enough
inventory − list of stock in a warehouse
fuel − material used to give power, e.g. coal, gas, etc.
stock level − quantity of goods kept in stock
furnace − large enclosed fire
spare part − small piece of machinery used to replace part of a machine which is broken
to run short of − to have too little or few of
cable − strong rope
pipe − tube used for carrying liquids and gas
to pack − to put items together for sending or selling
to wrap − to cover something with material, e.g. paper
pallet − flat wooden base on which goods can be stacked
to stack − to put things on top of each other

UNIT 21 **Project timing**

(prepositions of time)

1. Listening 🎧

Listen to the telephone conversation about the timing of a construction project. As you listen, complete the key for the project planner below.

Project Planner

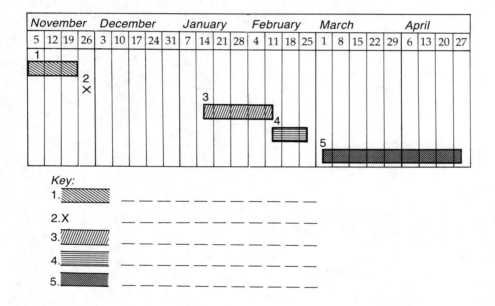

Key:
1. ───────────────────────
2. X ───────────────────────
3. ───────────────────────
4. ───────────────────────
5. ───────────────────────

2. Presentation

Notice how the following prepositions are used to refer to time:

on   days, dates, e.g.

       on 1 April, on Tuesday
       also
       on time = punctually

at   precise times, e.g.

at 6 o'clock, at 14.00
at the beginning/end
also
at the weekend
at night

in   periods of time, e.g.

in June, in 1987, in autumn, in the morning
also
in time = in sufficient time

by   a deadline (at the latest), e.g.

It must be finished by 18.00

Notice also these expressions which are used when talking about timing:

The project *is due to*   start on ...
             is expected to
             is scheduled to

3. Controlled practice

Complete these sentences with an appropriate preposition of time.
1. The work is due to begin _____ the end of April.
2. We are hoping to meet the engineer _____ the weekend.
3. We expect to sign the contract sometime _____ June.
4. We arrived _____ time to see them leave.
5. They are scheduled to finish _____ the middle of July.
6. I arranged to meet him _____ 15.30 _____ Tuesday.
7. The plane took off precisely _____ time.
8. We are busiest _____ spring.
9. The contract must be finalised _____ the end of the month.
10. He phoned me _____ one o'clock _____ night.

4. Transfer
PAIR WORK
Student B: Turn to the Key Section.
Student A: Ask Student B questions in order to complete the project planner overleaf.
             You should insert the following stages/events:

Key: 1. Preliminary study �▪

2. Contract negotiation X

3. Feasibility study ▪▪▪▪

4. Training ░░░░

5. Installation ⧄⧄⧄

6. Implementation date O

Project Planner

	January				February				March				April			
Wks	1	2	3	4	5	6	7	8	9	10	11	12	13	14	15	16

5. Word check

construction — building
project — plan
pilot study — test which, if successful, will be expanded into a full operation
to last — to take time
contractor — person or company which does work according to a written agreement
to schedule — to plan the time when something will happen
to sign — to write one's name on a document to approve or accept it
contract — legal agreement between two parties
stage — step
excavation — work of making a hole by digging
to sub-contract — to arrange that another company will do part of the work
foundations — base of a building put deep into the ground to support the walls
tight (of a schedule or timetable) — leaving no extra time at all to put right mistakes or difficulties

Factory tour

(prepositions of place)

---

1. Listening 🔘 —————————————————————————

A Plant Manager is showing some visitors around an electronic assembly plant. As you listen, match each object with the phrase describing its location.
 The first one has been done for you.

Object   *Location phrase*

SUPPLY AREA
 1. Raw materials   a. Takes them into supply room
 2. Conveyor   b. Stacked against the wall
 3. Components   c. Off-loaded onto a conveyor
 4. Boards   d. Stored between the boards and shelves
 5. Chemicals   e. Stored on shelves

ASSEMBLY AREA
 6. Boards   f. Come out of drilling machine
 7. Holes   g. Inserted into boards
 8. Boards   h. Pass through a cutter
 9. Components   i. Come off a conveyor
10. Boards   j. Drilled into boards

DESPATCH AREA
11. Assembled boards   k. Stacked in front of table
12. Despatch area   l. Sorted on this table
13. Boards   m. Go into despatch area
14. Boards   n. Packed in boxes
15. Boards   o. Behind this door

🔘

---

2. Presentation

Notice how the following prepositions are used to refer to place:

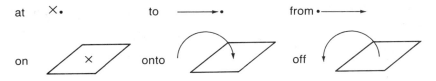

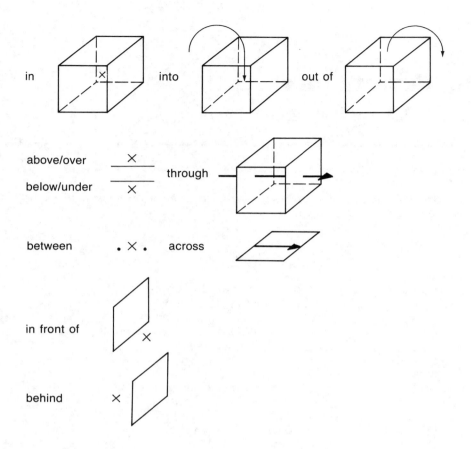

in

into

out of

above/over $\times$

below/under $\times$

through

between $\cdot\times\cdot$ across

in front of

behind $\times$

3. Controlled practice

Complete the following sentences with an appropriate preposition.

1. London lies _____ the River Thames.
2. I'll meet you _____ the airport. (*i.e. the terminal building*)
3. I'll meet you _____ the airport. (*i.e. that point on the map*)
4. (*looking at a map*) I can't find Tweedale Street at all. It must be _____ the map.
5. Cologne is _____ Bonn and Düsseldorf.
6. We walked _____ the main hall to a small room at the back.
7. My car is parked _____ _____ _____ the building.
8. Where's Peter? He just walked _____ _____ the office.
9. Come _____ my office. We can talk in private there.
10. On a clear day, you can see _____ the Channel _____ France.
11. Now I remember the bridge. It's _____ the River Avon.
12. Exhausted after the meeting, he dropped his briefcase _____ the desk.
13. He put the document _____ the safe.
14. I took the letter _____ the filing cabinet.
15. The ship sails _____ Hamburg _____ Stockholm.
16. The tunnel will be built 100 metres _____ sea level.

4. Transfer

PAIR WORK

Student B: Turn to the Key Section.

Student A: Complete the plan of an office to show where the following items of furniture are. Student B will tell you where they should be.

Items of furniture:
desk
telephone
safe
coat stand
filing cabinet
drinks cabinet
book shelves
meetings table
easy chairs

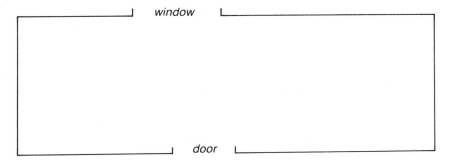

5. Word check

plant — factory
supply (area) — (place where) goods come before assembly
assembly (area) — (place where) items are put together from various parts
despatch (area) — (place from which) assembled items are sent to customers
raw materials — basic materials used to make finished products
truck — large motor vehicle for carrying goods
conveyor — moving belt for transport of products
storage — keeping in store
shelf — flat surface attached to a wall
component — part which will be put into a final product
to stack up — to put things on top of each other
board — long, thin, flat piece of solid material, e.g. wood
process — step or steps involved in manufacturing products in factories
shape — form
cutter — instrument for cutting
to drill — to make a hole or holes with a tool
to insert — to put in
to sort — to put in order according to size, etc.
to pack — to put things into a container for sending or selling

UNIT 23 **Market research**

(question formation)

---

1. Listening

A market researcher asks a consumer questions. As you listen, indicate whether the statements are true (T) or false (F). Write T or F in the right-hand column below.

T/F

1. The consumer is called Mrs J. Reynolds.
2. She lives at 21 Pine Avenue.
3. Her telephone number is 56822.
4. They rent their house.
5. Four people live in the house.
6. Both Mr and Mrs Reynolds work.
7. Her sons go to the local school.
8. They have two cars.
9. She drives about 5,000 miles a year.
10. They take two foreign holidays a year.
11. They usually go to the sea.
12. They spend about £1,000 on their summer holiday.
13. They plan to go to Greece this year.

---

2. Presentation

The market researcher used three different types of questions:

Wh-questions
Yes/No questions
Statement questions

Now look at the formation of these questions.

2.1 Direct questions

2.1.1 Wh-questions

Question word	auxiliary	subject	verb phrase
When		you/he/they etc.	take a holiday?
What car			drive?
Where	does/do	Mr Reynolds etc.	work?
Why			drive to work?
Which school		your children	go to?
How (many) children			have?

or

Question word	be	subject
How (old)	is/are	your son/children?

2.1.2 Yes/No questions

Auxiliary	subject	verb phrase
Does/do	you/he/they etc.	live in this house?

or

Be	subject	
Is/are	he/you/they	at school?

2.2 Statement questions

These are often used for *checking* information.

It's Mr and Mrs J. Reynolds, isn't it?
The address is 21 Pine Avenue? (*rising intonation*)
Your telephone number is 56822, is that right?

3. Controlled practice

You are doing a market research survey. You are interviewing a man called Mr P. Thomson. Ask questions as follows.

1. Check that his name is P. Thomson.

   _?

2. Check that his address is 45 Main Street.

   _?

3. Check that he owns his house.

— ?

4. Ask where he works.

— ?

5. Ask if he has worked there for long.

— ?

6. Ask how he travels to work.

— ?

7. As if he has any children.

— ?

8. Ask how old they are.

— ?

9. Ask if they are at school.

— ?

10. Ask what they do in the evenings.

— ?

11. Ask how often he goes to the cinema.

— ?

12. Ask if he ever goes to restaurants.

— ?

13. Ask when he goes to bed.

— ?

4. Transfer

GROUP WORK

You are the marketing team of a company which manufactures soap and hair shampoo. Your task is to design a questionnaire to find out what ideas consumers have for a new shampoo for women.

Your questionnaire should:

be aimed at shoppers in supermarkets
not take more than three minutes to answer

First decide what information you want to collect.
Then design the questionnaire.
Finally, try your questionnaire on other members of your class.

5. Word check

market researcher — person who examines the possible sales of a product before it is put on the market
consumer — person who buys and uses goods and services
personal — private
to own — to have, to possess
roughly — about
firm — company
abroad — in/to another country
to suppose — to estimate
actually — in fact

The budget meeting

(modals)

---

1. Listening ⟨oo⟩

Listen to the extract from a budget meeting. Peter, John and Susan are discussing next year's departmental budgets. As you listen, indicate their opinions in the table below.
  Use these symbols:

+   = more money should be spent
−   = less money should be spent
OK = the proposed figure should remain the same

Budget proposals

Department	Budget	Peter	John	Susan
Research	£25,000			
Marketing	£45,000			
Production	£145,000			
Sales	£55,000			

⟨oo⟩

2. Presentation

Modals can be used to indicate speakers' attitudes or opinions. These can be categorised as follows:

strong recommendation
possibility
slight possibility
impossibility

Now look at the modals used to express opinions in the meeting.

2.1 Strong recommendation

1. to do something
   We *should* increase the research budget.
   Production *ought to* manage with less.
2. not to do something
   The figure *shouldn't* be changed.

2.2 Possibility

We *could* reduce the figure for marketing.

2.3 Slight possibility

We *might* save a bit on after-sales.

2.4 Impossibility

We *can't* cut the production budget.

Notice how the *strength* of the opinion can be varied by using these modal verbs.

3. Controlled practice

Use the language above to transform these sentences. The first one has been done for you.

1. I strongly recommend we reduce the sales budget.
   We should/ought to reduce the sales budget.

2. There's a small chance that marketing would accept a cut in their budget.
   Marketing _ _ _ _ _ _ _ _ _ _ _ _ _ _ _.

3. A cut in the production budget is out of the question.
   We _ _ _ _ _ _ _ _ _ _ _ _ _ _ _.

4. It's possible to spend more on direct sales activities.
   We _ _ _ _ _ _ _ _ _ _ _ _ _ _ _.

5. It is advisable to reduce the total budget.
   We _ _ _ _ _ _ _ _ _ _ _ _ _ _ _.

6. It's impossible for research to continue on this budget.
   Research _ _ _ _ _ _ _ _ _ _ _ _ _ _ _.

7. There is a possibility that more money will be made available.
   More money _ _ _ _ _ _ _ _ _ _ _ _ _ _ _.

8. I strongly recommend we do not cut the marketing budget.
   We _ _ _ _ _ _ _ _ _ _ _ _ _ _ _.

9. There's a small chance sales will not reach their target.
   Sales _ _ _ _ _ _ _ _ _ _ _ _ _ _ _.

10. Production will possibly need more money later in the year.
    Production _ _ _ _ _ _ _ _ _ _ _ _ _ _ _.

4. Transfer

GROUP WORK

What do you think?

Give your opinions about the following:

1. We should all learn just one language.
2. Money spent on space research is a waste.
3. A career in public service (education, etc.) is more valuable than a career in business.
4. The most important resource of all companies is people.

Here are some examples to start you off:

A: I think we should all learn one language.
B: Why should we do that?
A: Well, then we could communicate better.
B: But if everyone could communicate better, we might lose some of our existing customers.
A: I don't see why.
B: Well, they could probably buy the same goods somewhere else more cheaply.

5. Word check

budget – plan of expected spending and income
opinion – idea
to propose – to suggest
proposal – suggestion
to reduce – to make less or smaller
to allow – to make it possible for someone to do something
to increase – to make more or bigger
launch – act of putting a new product on the market
mid-year – in the middle of the year
to cut – to reduce
investment – money usefully spent
to save – not to spend money
after-sales (service) – service of a machine carried out by the seller for some time after the machine has been bought
out of the question – not for discussion, unacceptable

UNIT 25 **Financial control**

(modals of obligation)

---

1. Listening 〔oo〕 ————————————

The Managing Director, Financial Controller and Personnel Manager are discussing ways of tightening financial control and reducing costs. As you listen, decide whether the statements are true (T) or false (F) by writing 'T' or 'F' in the right-hand column.

Statements   *T/F*
The MD feels they must tighten up on financial control.
The Financial Controller feels they have got to reduce payment times.
They must reduce payment times to 30 days.
They must get tough with their customers.
Their suppliers must help them.
The Personnel Manager feels they don't have to cut training and
   personnel development.
The Managing Director feels they must reduce costs.
The Managing Director feels they have got to stop some existing
   training.
Both the Managing Director and the Personnel Manager have to leave
   for other meetings.

—————————————————————————————— 〔oo〕

2. Presentation

Now look at the language used in the meeting to express:

obligation to do something
prohibition
lack of obligation

2.1 Obligation

We *must* reduce costs   (*our internal obligation*)
i.e. Our Chairman has told us to do so
We *have to* reduce costs   (*an external obligation we must accept*)
i.e. Customers have told us to do so
We*'ve got to* reduce costs   (*informal*)

2.2 Prohibition

We *mustn't* cut the training budget

2.3 Lack of obligation

We *don't have to* get tough with customers.

3. Controlled practice

Transform these sentences using the language presented above. All the sentences should begin: 'We _ _ _ _ _'.
 The first one has been done for you.

1. It is essential we do not expand too fast.
   We mustn't expand too fast. __

2. It is not necessary to enter export markets yet.
   _.

3. It is absolutely vital we discuss this at the next meeting.
   _.

4. We can't avoid firing him. He can no longer do his job.
   _.

5. There is no obligation to pay the Christmas bonus.
   _.

6. It is forbidden to enter this part of the building.
   _.

7. It is essential that we leave now.

   —.

8. It doesn't matter if we don't catch that plane.

   —.

9. It's very important we do not miss the 18.00 plane.

   —.

10. It's vital we increase our turnover.

   —.

4. Transfer
GROUP WORK

Discuss the following business problems and decide what action you must/mustn't/don't have to take.

1. An employee is always late for work. You have told him once that this cannot continue.
2. A very big customer of yours is a very late payer. You sometimes wait more than three months for payment.
3. A colleague at work has got personal problems. He is not able to concentrate at work.
4. You think your salary is too low. You have not had an increase for three years.
5. All your colleagues finish work at 17.30. You have been given a lot of extra work. You never finish before 19.00.

5. Word check

to tighten (up) − to control more effectively
control − strict management of activities of a department (especially Finance)
to reduce − to make less or smaller
credit − time given to a customer before he must pay
delay − when something is later than planned
invoice − note asking for payment for goods or services supplied
to argue − to discuss something about which you do not agree
reminder − letter to remind a customer that he has not paid an invoice
supplier − person or company which provides goods or services
measures − steps
support − which help (somebody or something to be more effective)
to cut − to reduce
investment − placing of money so that it will increase the value of the company
budget − plan of expected spending
limited − restricted, small in amount
worthwhile − worth doing

KEY SECTION   Units 1–25

This section contains:

i   tapescripts and keys to the Listening exercises
ii   answers to the Controlled practice exercises
iii information for the Transfer section where required

First meetings 1

1. Listening 🔊

Tapescript

1. A: Hello, let me introduce myself. My name's Klein, Günther Klein.
   B: Pleased to meet you. I'm Geoff Snowdon.
2. A: How do you do? My name's Paul Matthews.
   B: Nice to meet you. Mine's Akira Mishima.
3. A: Hello, I'm Tom.
   B: Nice to meet you. My name's Francine.
4. A: Peter, could you introduce me to the Marketing Manager?
   B: Of course John. ... Philip, let me introduce you to John, our new Computer Manager.
   C: Nice to meet you John, we're going to be working together.
5. A: Herr Tübingen, I haven't met your Managing Director yet.
   B: Oh, I'm sorry. Come and meet him. Dr Mannheim, this is Mr Roberts. He's over from the States on a visit.
   C: Very nice to meet you, Mr Roberts. How long are you here for?
6. A: Jane, I don't know anyone here. You'll have to introduce me.
   B: Of course, I'll introduce you to Roger first. He's the host. ... Roger, this is Susan. She's just moved to the area.
   C: Nice to meet you, Susan. Do you come from these parts?
7. A: Let me introduce you two. Maxine, this is Francis.
   B: Nice to meet you, Maxine. Are you an old friend of Tony's?
   C: Oh yes, Tony and I have known each other for years, haven't we?
   A: Yes, that's right.

Answers to the listening task

1st person	*2nd person*	*3rd person*
Günther Klein	Mr Roberts	
Paul Matthews	John	Philip
Tom	Geoff Snowdon	Francis
Peter	Maxine	Dr Mannheim
Herr Tübingen	Francine	Roger
Jane	Akira Mishima	
Tony	Susan	

Introduction 1	(F)		Introduction 5	(F)
Introduction 2	(F)		Introduction 6	(I)
Introduction 3	(I)		Introduction 7	(I)
Introduction 4	(I)			

🔊

3. Controlled practice

1. PETER KING: Hello, *let me introduce myself*. My name's Peter King.
   JACK SIMPSON: *Nice/Pleased to meet you*. I'm Jack Simpson.
2. SARAH: Philip, I *don't know anyone* here. You'll have to *introduce me*.
   PHILIP: Of *course*, I'll *introduce you* to James. He's an old friend of mine. James, *this is* Sarah, she's just joined the company.
   JAMES: *(Very) nice to meet you*, Sarah. Where do you come from?
3. PETE: Rod, *I haven't met* Mr Rogers, the Purchasing Manager from Kentons.
   ROD: I'm *sorry*. Come and meet him. Mr Rogers, *let me introduce you to* Pete Taylor, our Export Sales Manager.
   MR ROGERS: *(Very) nice to meet you*. What countries do you cover?
4. KLAUS FISCHER: How *do you do?* My *name's Klaus Fischer*.
   AMERICAN: *Pleased/Nice to meet you*. *Mine's* George Cole.

UNIT 2 **First meetings 2**

1. Listening 🔘

Tapescript

Dialogue 1
A: Nice to meet you, Peter. What do you do for a living?
B: I'm in computers — software development. What about you, John?
A: Oh, I work for Manders — in the Personnel Department. Not a bad job.
B: Is that one of your colleagues over there?
A: Yes, that's Susan. She works in the Accounts Department. Let me introduce you.

Dialogue 2
A: Hello, I'm Mike.
B: Nice to meet you. I'm Sarah. I haven't seen you around before.
A: No, I've just started work for Manders. I'm in the Sales Department.
B: What do you do there?
A: Oh, I'm on the market research side. And you?
B: Well, I've been with Manders for years. I'm Mr Field's Personal Assistant. He's the Sales Director.
A: Ah, I haven't met him. Is he here?
B: Yes, that's him. Let me introduce you.

Dialogue 3
A: That's interesting. Do you work here, Martin?
B: Yes, I'm in Finance. What about you, Jean?
A: Well, my husband works at Manders. He's in the Production Department.
B: Oh yes, I think I've met him. What about you? Do you work?

A: Yes, I'm a fashion designer. I work from home.
B: That's interesting.

Answers to the listening task

1. c	4. d	7. i
2. f	5. b	8. e
3. g	6. h	9. a

── ⟦◯◯⟧

3. Controlled practice

A
1. What do you do *for* a living?
2. I work *for/with/at* Manders.
3. I work *in* the Personnel Department.
4. I'm *on* the recruitment side.
5. I'm *in* fashion design.
6. He's *in* the Production Department.
7. I work *from/at* home.
8. She's been *with/at* Manders for years.

B
1. I'm in computers. What about you?
2. I'm Mr Jones secretary. He's the Production Manager.
3. I live in Paris. What about you?
4. My husband's in the Production Department.
5. Hello, I'm Sarah. I haven't seen you around before.

(b) *Well, I work in Sales.*
(c) *Oh, I haven't met him.*

(b) *Well, I come from the North.*
(c) *Oh yes, I think I've met him.*
(c) *No, I'm new here.*

4. Transfer
PAIR WORK
Student B: Below are three business cards. Use the information to practise three introductory conversations about jobs and places of work.

```
┌──────────────────────────────────────────┐
│  Nixon Computers                          │
│  James Fox, Software Development Section   │
│                                            │
│  432 Ocean Boulevard, Los Angeles         │
│  Tel: 4-657889   Telex: Nix 677001        │
└──────────────────────────────────────────┘
```

```
┌─────────────────────────────────────────────────────────┐
│  Persson Chemicals                                        │
│  Anders Jonsson, Research & Development Manager           │
│                                                           │
│  544 Konigsgatan, Stockholm, Sweden                       │
│  Tel: 8-6774 342   Telex: 67742                           │
│  Home: 32 Micklegatan, Uppsala                            │
│                                                           │
└─────────────────────────────────────────────────────────┘
```

```
┌─────────────────────────────────────────────────────────┐
│  Fiser Pharmaceuticals                                    │
│  Jurgen Wolff, Product Manager                            │
│  Friedrichstrasse 43, München      Tel: 765-674-887       │
│                                                           │
└─────────────────────────────────────────────────────────┘
```

UNIT 3 **First contact**

---

1. Listening ⟨oo⟩ ──────────────────────────────

Dialogue 1
— Is this your first trip to Japan?
— Yes, it is.
— Do you like it here?
— Yes, it seems interesting.
— Would you like another drink?
— Thank you.

Dialogue 2
— How was your trip?
— Fine thanks.
— How do you find Tokyo?
— Very interesting.
— Which hotel are you staying in?
— The Sheraton.

Dialogue 3
— Is this your first trip to Japan?
— Yes, but hopefully not my last.
— I'm pleased to hear that. Have you found time to see much?
— Well, I visited the gardens.
— Oh, are you interested in gardens?
— Actually yes, it's my hobby.
— Mine too . . .

Dialogue 4
— Are you staying long?
— No, unfortunately only a couple of weeks.
— Business or pleasure?
— Business I'm afraid. My company is setting up an office here in Tokyo.
— Really, where is your company based?
— In Detroit, sort of north mid-west of the States.
— Yes, I know it. I visited it two years ago.
— Ah, really? . . .

Dialogue 5
— I believe you're in fashion.
— Yes that's right — on the design side.
— That's a coincidence. My wife's a fashion designer.
— Oh, I'd like to meet her.
— You must come round to dinner one evening.
— That would be nice.
— Good, I'll fix it up later this week.

Answers to the listening task

	Successful	*Unsuccessful*
Dialogue 1:		X
Dialogue 2:		X
Dialogue 3:	√	
Dialogue 4:	√	
Dialogue 5:	√	

Dialogue 1: Has the visitor been to Japan before? *No*
Dialogue 2: Which hotel is the visitor staying in? *Sheraton*
Dialogue 3: What topic of common interest do they find? *Gardens*
Dialogue 4: What topic of common interest do they find? *Detroit*
Dialogue 5: What topic of common interest do they find? *Fashion*

3. Controlled practice

Dialogue 1
— Is this your first trip over here?
— No, I've been to the States before, but this is the first time in Atlanta.
— So what do you think of Atlanta?
— Well, it's not what I expected.

- Really? What did you expect?
- Well, I suppose I thought it would be more traditional.
- There is a part like that. You must let me show you around.
- That would be interesting.
- Fine, I'll see what I can arrange.

Dialogue 2
- Are you staying long?
- No, just a couple of days.
- That's a pity. There's a lot to see.
- I'm sure. I hope to get back here again.
- Good. Are you here on business then?
- Yes, we're thinking of setting up an office here.
- Really? That's interesting. What line are you in?

Dialogue 3
- I believe you're in journalism.
- Yes, that's right — on the editorial side.
- That's interesting. My son is an editor on the local paper.
- Really? I expect I'll meet him.
- Yes, what about coming round for a drink? I could introduce you to him.
- That would be nice.

Dialogue 4
- How do you find the weather here?
- A bit warmer than back home.
- Oh, so where do you come from?
- Scotland. This time of year it's pretty cold.
- I can imagine. I've never been but people tell me it's very beautiful.
- Yes, that's right. The best time to visit is in the summer.
- Maybe I'll get across next year.
- Well, if you do come across, you must visit us.

UNIT 4 **Further contact**

1. Listening 🔘

Tapescript

1. Thanks for the lovely evening. → Glad you enjoyed it.
2. How about a drink? → Don't mention it.
3. Do you mind if I smoke? → Yes, I do.
4. Could you hand me that pen? → Of course. Here you are.
5. My father died last night. → Oh, I am sorry to hear that.
6. Have a good weekend. → So do I.
7. Thanks for your help. → Never mind.

8. I'm sorry, I must have got the wrong number. → It doesn't matter.
9. Best of luck in your new job. → Not at all.
10. He's 95, you know! → Really?
11. I think we should leave now. → So do I.
12. We've had a very good year. → I'm glad to hear that.
13. Can I ask you a question? → Don't mention it.
14. Would you like to go to a concert this evening? → Yes, I'd love to.
15. I didn't get the job. → That's true.

Answers to the listening task

1. √	6. X	11. √
2. X	7. X	12. √
3. X	8. √	13. X
4. √	9. X	14. √
5. √	10. √	15. X

Appropriate responses

1. Thanks for the lovely evening. → Glad you enjoyed it.
2. How about a drink? → That would be nice.
3. Do you mind if I smoke? → No, of course not.
4. Could you hand me that pen? → Of course. Here you are.
5. My father died last night. → Oh, I am sorry to hear that.
6. Have a good weekend. → You too.
7. Thanks for your help. → You're welcome.
8. I'm sorry, I must have got the wrong number. → It doesn't matter.
9. Best of luck in your new job. → Thanks very much.
10. He's 95, you know! → Really?
11. I think we should leave now. → So do I.
12. We've had a very good year. → I'm glad to hear that.
13. Can I ask you a question? → Yes, of course.
14. Would you like to go to a concert this evening? → Yes, I'd love to.
15. I didn't get the job. → Never mind. Better luck next time.

─── ▭◯◯

3. Controlled practice

1. We lost the match. → *Never mind. Better luck next time.*
2. Do you mind if I open the window? → *No, of course not.*
3. Would you like to go to a concert this evening? → *Yes, I'd love/like to.*
4. Sorry, I interrupted you. → *It doesn't matter/Don't worry/Never mind.*
5. Could you pass me the file? → *Of course. Here you are.*
6. I hope he gets the job. → *So do I/Me too/I hope so too.*
7. Have a good Christmas. → *You too/Same to you.*
8. She's only 18 and she's already married with two children! → *Really?*
9. I think it's going to rain. → *Me too/So do I/I think so too.*
10. Thanks. That was a delicious meal. → *Glad you liked/enjoyed it.*

11. My car broke down again this morning. → *I am sorry to hear that/Hard luck.*
12. Can I see you for a moment? → *Yes, of course/Certainly.*
13. How about something to eat? → *That would be nice/That's a good idea.*
14. You must come round for dinner. → *I'd love/like to.*
15. I'm sorry. I've taken the wrong file. → *Don't worry/Never mind/It doesn't matter.*

4. Transfer
PAIR WORK

Student B: Respond appropriately when Student A thanks, apologises, requests permission, etc.

Then you yourself should thank, apologise, etc., and Student A should respond appropriately.

UNIT 5 Company organisation

1. Listening ⌾

Tapescript

I'd like to say a few words about the organisational structure of Rossomon. Now, if you look at the transparency you will see that the Managing Director, that is Mr Bunce, is responsible for running the company and is accountable to the Board.

Now, he is assisted by four executive departments. These are Human Resources, which is responsible for personnel, training and management development; then there is the Finance Department which takes care of corporate finance and accounting; next we have the Management Services Departmen, led by Peter Jenkins who is in charge of rationalisation throughout the company; and finally there is the R & D Department — research and development — which works closely with the five regions on new product development.

So this then brings me on to the regions. Directly under the Managing Director, there are five Regional Managers. Each of them is responsible for the day-to-day management of a territory — these are geographically split into North, South, East, West and Central Regions.

Now then, the five regions are supported by two sections — Marketing and Technical Services. They are organised on a matrix basis with section leaders accountable to the Regional Managers. They work closely with the regions on the marketing and technical side.

Now, in addition to the parent company, Rossomon has three subsidiaries, namely Rossomon France, Germany and Japan. The subsidiaries report to the Export Sales Department, which in turn is accountable to the Board.

Right, well that's a brief overview. Are there any questions?

Answers to the listening task

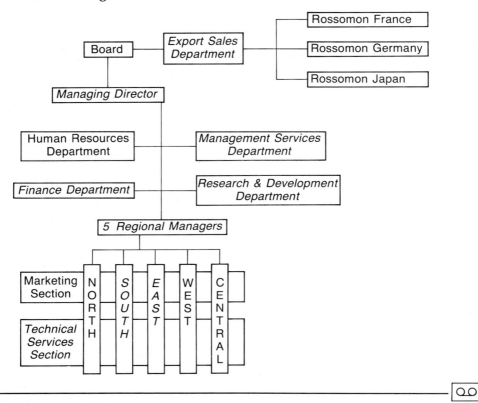

---

3. Controlled practice

1. The Managing Director *reports/is accountable* to the Board.
2. The Managing Director *is responsible* for running the company.
3. The Managing Director *is supported/is assisted* by four executive departments.
4. *Under* the Managing Director, there are five regional divisions.
5. Each Regional Manager *is in charge* of a territory.
6. The five regions *are supported/are assisted* by two other sections − Marketing and Technical Services.
7. The Section Leaders *report to/are accountable* to the Regional Managers.
8. In addition to the *parent* company, Rossomon has three *subsidiaries*: Rossomon France, Germany and Japan.
9. The subsidiaries *report/are accountable* to the Export Sales Department.
10. The Export Sales Department is *accountable* to the Board.

4. Transfer

1. **Student B:** Listen to Student A's description of the typical management structure of a British company. Use the information to complete the organisation chart below.

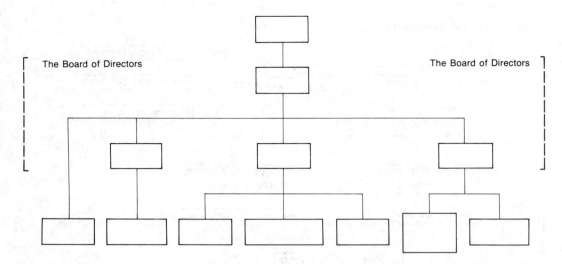

2. Now describe the typical management structure of an American company:

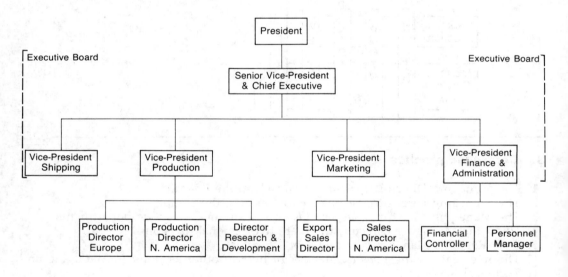

UNIT 6 Supply

1. Listening 🔊

Tapescript

A: Good morning. I'm phoning to enquire about your office shelving system ... code number SS007.

B: Oh yes, what would you like to know?

A: Well, I'd like to check on the dimensions first — make sure that they'll fit. First of all, how wide are they?

B: Just a moment sir, I'll get the specifications ... you asked about the width ... yes, the standard unit is 3.5 metres wide.

A: And the height?

B: They're 2 metres high with flexible positions for the shelves.

A: How many shelves can actually be fitted?

B: Really as many as you like, but normally five.

A: I see. I need to know how much they stick out — in other words, how deep are they?

B: They're 30 centimetres deep.

A: Thanks, that's the dimensions. Now, what about delivery?

B: Well, it depends how far you are from our warehouse.

A: We're about ten miles from the centre.

B: I see — well, that's in our free delivery area, so there'll be no extra charge for delivery.

A: Good. Actually, what I meant was how long does it take after I place an order?

B: I see sir. We guarantee delivery within two weeks.

A: Good. Well, we're interested in ten of your standard units for a suite of offices. How much do you charge?

B: Well the unit cost is £98 but in view of the size of the order, we can offer a 5 per cent discount ... just a moment, I'll just do the figures ... yes, that comes to £931 — let's round it off and call it £930.

A: That sounds reasonable. Finally, what sort of guarantee do you offer?

B: Well, these units are extremely sturdy and reliable. There's the usual one-year guarantee but they have an average life of at least 20 years ...

Answers to the listening task

Dimensions	Width	3.5 m
	Height	2.0 m
	Depth	30 cm
Delivery:	Cost	No charge
	Time	Two weeks
Price:	Unit price	£98
	Discount price	£930 for 10 units
Guarantee period		One year
Average life		At least 20 years

3. Controlled practice

A

Noun form	adjective	opposite adjective
Width	wide	narrow
Length	long	short
Depth	deep	shallow
Height	high	low
Distance	far	near
Speed	fast	slow
Reliability	reliable	unreliable

B
1. The width of the printer: *How wide is it?*
2. The depth of the printer: *How deep is it?*
3. The speed of the printer: *How fast is it?*
4. The time to deliver: *How long does it take to deliver?*
5. The cost of delivery: *How much is it/does it cost/do you charge to deliver?*
6. The reliability of the printer: *How reliable is it?*
7. The length of the cable: *How long is the cable?*
8. The length of the guarantee period: *How long is the guarantee (period)?*
9. The cost of the printer: *How much does it cost/is it?*
10. The distance to the nearest service centre: *How far is (it to) the nearest service centre?*

4. Transfer
PAIR WORK
Student B: Student A is going to ask you about the typewriter below. Answer the questions about the product features according to the information given.

Dimensions:	w	28 cm
	d	30 cm
	h	8 cm
Delivery:	time	28 days
	cost	no charge
Price:	for one	£75
	for more than five	£67.50
Guarantee period:		one year

UNIT 7 Travel information

1. Listening 🔘

Tapescript

Dialogue 1
A: Could you tell me when the first plane for Hamburg leaves?
B: At seven in the morning.
A: And what time does it arrive?
B: At 9.15.
A: Thank you.
B: You're welcome.

Dialogue 2
A: Do you happen to know where the airport bus leaves from?
B: No, I'm sorry. I can't help you.
A: Excuse me, do you happen to know where the airport bus stops?
C: Yes, I think it goes from outside the central railway station.
A: Thank you.

Dialogue 3
A: Could you tell me what platform the train leaves from?
B: Yes, it's platform 12.
A: Thank you, which end of the station is that?
B: It's at the right-hand end.
A: Thanks.

Dialogue 4
A: Could you tell me whether there are any sleeping compartments on the train?
B: I'm sorry, sir. None on this train.
A: Is there a dining car then?
B: Yes, you'll find it in the centre of the train.
A: Thank you.

Answers to the listening task

Dialogue 1
Departure time of first plane to Hamburg: *07.00*
Arrival time at Hamburg: *09.15*

Dialogue 2
Departure place of airport bus: *outside the central railway station*

Dialogue 3
Platform number: *12*
End of station: *right-hand end*

Dialogue 4
Number of sleeping compartments on train: *none*
Location of dining car on train: *in the centre of the train*

---

3. Controlled practice

A
1. The time of the first train to Rome.
   Could you tell me when the first train to Rome leaves?
2. The platform the train leaves from.
   Could you tell me which platform it leaves from?
3. The arrival time in Rome.
   Could you tell me when it arrives in Rome?
4. If there is a dining car.
   Could you tell me whether/if there is a dining car?
5. If there are any sleeping compartments.
   Could you tell me whether/if there are any sleeping compartments?

B
1. The name of this street.
   Do you happen to know (what) the name of this street (is)?
2. If there is a tourist information office in the town.
   Do you happen to know whether/if there is a tourist information office in the town?
3. The time the banks open.
   Do you happen to know when the banks open?
4. The location of the underground car park.
   Do you happen to know where the underground car park is?
5. The location of the nearest chemist.
   Do you happen to know where the nearest chemist is?

C
1. If you have to change trains.
   Do I/we have to change trains?

2. If platform 5 is the right platform for the train to Milan.
   Is platform 5 (the) right (platform) for the train to Milan?
3. The departure time of the last train to Zürich.
   When does the last train to Zürich leave?
4. The position in the train of the first class compartments.
   Where/Which end are the first class compartments?
5. The best route to the airport.
   Which is/What's the best route to the airport?

4. Transfer

1. **Student B:** You want to find out about flights from Paris to London. You go to a travel agency and ask the assistant (Student A) for the following information:

   the time of the first plane to Paris
   the arrival time
   if there is a flight at 12.00
   the terminal numbers for these flights
   the check-in time for these flights

2. **Student B:** You are a visitor to London. You stop a stranger in the street and ask for the following information:

   how to get to London Heathrow
   the journey time from London to the airport

3. **Student B:** You work in a railway information office. Use the following information to answer Student A's questions.

Trains from **London (Victoria Station)** to **Paris (Gare du Nord)** using Channel Tunnel	
Dep. time	Arr. time
06.00	10.30
07.00	11.30
09.00	12.30
NOTES: All trains require seat reservations.	

4. **Student B:** You are in the street. Somebody (Student A) stops you to ask for the following information:

   the nearest bus stop — just across the street
   the time of the next bus to Victoria — you don't know
   if you have to give the driver the exact fare — yes

105

UNIT 8 **Making arrangements**

1. Listening

Tapescript

Call 1
A: Krondike Electronics. Can I help you?
B: Yes, I'd like to speak to Mr Edwards, please.
A: Who's calling, please?
B: John Bird.
A: Just a moment Mr Bird; I'll put you through.
C: Miss Taylor speaking.
B: John Bird here. Can I speak to Mr Edwards?
C: I'm afraid he's out at the moment. Can I take a message?
B: Yes, could you ask him to call me back as soon as possible?
C: Yes, of course. Could I have your number?
B: He's got it, but just in case, it's 01-253 4686.
C: 01-253 4686. Thank you Mr Bird. I'll make sure he gets the message.
B: Thank you. Bye.
C: Goodbye.

Call 2
A: John Bird speaking.
B: This is Pete Edwards. My secretary said you called.
A: Yes, that's right. Thanks for getting back. Look, the reason I called was we're having installation problems with the E 258.
B: Really, that surprises me. What sort of problems?
A: Well, it's a bit complicated. Could you send a technician round?
B: Of course, I'll get one round this afternoon.
A: That would be great.
B: OK, I'm sure we'll sort it out in no time. Bye.
A: Goodbye.

Call 3
A: Pearson and Brown. Can I help you?
B: This is Gerald Smith from Taylor & Sons. Could I speak to Mrs Phillips?
A: Just a moment, Mr Smith, I'll put you through.
C: Susan Phillips speaking.
B: Hello Susan. This is Gerald Smith.
C: Oh hello Gerald. How are you?
B: Fine. I'm just phoning to see if we could fix a meeting for next week.
C: Yes, of course. We've got to discuss next year's order. Just a moment, I'll get my diary ... Right, next week ...?
B: Could you manage Tuesday?
C: I'm sorry. I'm out all day on Tuesday.
B: What about Friday then?
C: Yes Friday in the morning would suit me fine.
B: Good, that suits me too. Shall we say 10 o'clock?
C: Fine. So 10 o'clock here then?

B: Yes, that's probably easiest. Right, I look forward to seeing you.
C: Bye.
B: Bye.

Answers to the listening task

Call	Name of person called	Name of caller	Reason for call	Result of call
1	Mr Edwards	John Bird	///////////////	Edwards to call Bird back
2	John Bird	Pete Edwards	Installation problems	Technician to go round in the afternoon
3	Susan Phillips	Gerald Smith	To fix a meeting	Meeting arranged 10.00 next Friday

3. Controlled practice

A
1. — Pan Electronics. Can I help you?
   — Yes, I'd like to speak to Miss Rathbone.
   — Who's calling, please?
   — Peter Jones.
   — Just a moment, Mr Jones, I'll put you through.

2. — Mr Gottman here. Could I speak to Mrs Fields?
   — I'm afraid she's out at the moment. Can I take a message?
   — Yes, could you ask her to call me back?
   — Yes, of course. Could I have your number?
   — She's got it, but just in case, it's 01-253 4686.

3. — Just a moment, I'll get my diary . . . you said next week.
   — Yes, could you manage Wednesday?
   — I'm sorry, I'm out on Wednesday.
   — What about Thursday then?
   — Yes, Thursday morning would suit me fine.
   — Good, that suits me too. Shall we say 11 o'clock?

B
1. John Peterson speaking.   (c) *Hello, John. This is Peter Matthews.*
2. Can I take a message?   (b) *Yes, could you ask him to call me back?*
3. The reason I called is we're having problems.   (b) *Really? That surprises me.*
4. Could you manage Tuesday?   (c) *I'm afraid I can't.*
5. So that's fixed — Friday at 11 o'clock.   (b) *Right, I look forward to seeing you then.*

4. Transfer

PAIR WORK

Student B: 1. You are Mr/s Rogers' secretary. Mr/s Rogers is out. You will receive a call from Student A. Take a message: Make sure you get his/her name and telephone number.

2. You are Mr/s Rogers. Call Student A back. He/she will want to know the discount price for ten pairs of shoes.
   Normal price: £19 per pair
   Discount: 10%

3. You are Mr/s Dunn. Student A will call you to arrange a meeting next week. Below is your diary for next week:

	Monday	Tuesday	Wednesday	Thursday	Friday
morning		T R A D E	Trade Fair finishes 11.00 12.30 train to London		Z U R I C H
afternoon	Lunch with Marketing Manager Go to Leeds for Trade Fair Hotel Imperial	F A I R	Meeting with client: 14.00–15.30	Plane to Zurich BA 671 	Plane to London SA 897 dep: 15.30

UNIT 9 Information handling

1. Listening 📼

Tapescript

A: Priority Investments. Can I help you?

B: Yes, this is George Biederbeke. Could I speak to someone in your corporate finance department?

A: Just a moment, I'll put you through.

C: Daniels speaking.

B: My name is George Biederbeke from the Austin Corporation. I'd like to make an appointment to see your Corporate Finance Manager.

C: Yes. Could you tell me what exactly you want to talk about?
B: Well, we're approaching a number of investment companies with a view to placing business with them.
C: I'm sorry, I didn't quite catch that.
B: I said that we are interested in your investment services.
C: I see, and you would like to meet our Corporate Finance Manager?
B: That's right.
C: When would be convenient for you?
B: Friday 28 June would suit me — in the afternoon.
C: Just a moment, I'll check with Mr Foster — our Corporate Finance Manager.
B: I'm sorry, I didn't catch his name.
C: Foster.
B: Right.
C: Just a moment, let me check . . . Yes, that'll be fine, about 2 p.m. Could I have your name again?
B: Biederbeke.
C: Could you spell that please?
B: B, I, E, D, E, R, B, E, K, E.
C: Right, I've got that. We'd like to send you a copy of our current prospectus. If you give me your address . . .
B: Of course. It's the Austin Corporation, 514 Seaview . . .
C: 514 Seanew.
B: No, it's Sea — view.
C: Right, I've got that.
B: 2952 Seattle.
C: 2952 Seattle. Right, let me just repeat that. Mr Biederbeke, Austin Corporation, 514 Seaview, 2952 Seattle.
B: Right.
C: And your telephone number, Mr Biederbeke?
B: It's (0452) 67791.
C: (0452) 67791. Right. We'll get the prospectus in the post to you today.
B: Good. Let me just confirm the appointment. Friday 28 June at 2 o'clock.
C: Fine, we look forward to seeing you then.
B: Goodbye.
C: Goodbye.

Answers to the listening task

First listening

Caller's notes:
Name of Company: Priority Investments
Name of Corporate Finance Manager: *Mr Foster*
Date of appointment: *Friday 28 June*
Time of appointment: *14.00*

Second listening

Called person's notes:
Caller's name: *Mr Biederbeke*
Caller's company: *Austin Corporation*
Caller's address: *514 Seaview, 2952 Seattle*

Tel: No.: *(0452) 67791*
Reason for call: *Meeting with Mr Foster to discuss investment services*
Date of appointment: *Friday 28 June*
Time of appointment: *14.00*
Action: 1. Confirm appointment with Mr Foster.
  2. Send *prospectus to Mr Biederbeke.*

⎯⎯⎯⎯⎯⎯⎯⎯⎯⎯⎯⎯⎯⎯⎯⎯⎯⎯⎯⎯⎯⎯⎯⎯⎯ 〔ᴑᴑ〕

3. Controlled practice

A
1. My name's Pinkerton.
 Could you spell that please?
 Yes, it's P, I, N, K, E, R, T, O, N.
2. The address is 24 Tunnyside Lane.
 Could you repeat that?
 Yes, of course. 24 Tunnyside Lane.
3. My phone number is 0432-5686.
 0432-5688.
 No, it's 5686.
 Let me just repeat that — 0432-5686.
 That's right.
4. I'd like an appointment with Mr Dunn.
 Could you tell me exactly what you would like to discuss?
 Yes, I'd like to talk about extending my credit.
5. We would like to visit your factory with a view to buying it.
 I see. When would you like to come?
6. The figure is 3.56 m.
 I've got that. And what was the other figure?
7. So an appointment at two would suit you. *Could I have your name* again, please?
 Yes, certainly, it's Macintosh.
 Could you spell that?
 Yes, M, A, C, I, N, T, O, S, H.

B
1. 0232-77551
2. 010−35−444−7889
3. 08−674−5500
4. 00−44−904−24246
5. 1−775−9191
6. 010−49−214−30761

C
Names:
1. Peterson. Could you spell that please?
 P, e, t, e, r, s, o, n.
2. Hardy. Could you spell that please?
 H, a, r, d, y.
3. Glynis. Could you spell that please?
 G, l, y, n, i, s.
4. Matthews. Could you spell that please?
 M, a, t, t, h, e, w, s.
5. Rifkind. Could you spell that please?
 R, i, f, k, i, n, d.

6. Thatcher. Could you spell that please?
   T, h, a, t, c, h, e, r.
7. Samuel. Could you spell that please?
   S, a, m, u, e, l.
8. Marjorie. Could you spell that please?
   M, a, r, j, o, r, i, e.

4. Transfer

Student B: 1. You will receive a phone call from Student A (ABC Sports). You are
Mr Savary. You represent Newsome Sports Ltd. You have placed an order
with ABC Sports as follows:

Name of your company: Newsome Sports & Co.
Address: 25 Margate Hill, London NW11.
Tel: 01-785 8855   Telex: Not available

Order: 50 pairs of training shoes
　　　　30 pairs of socks
　　　　12 Greys Squash rackets
Delivery date: 5.10.88 or earlier
Price: training shoes − £13.00 per pair
　　　　socks − £3.00 per pair
　　　　squash rackets − £20.00 per racket

2. You work for Skiwear UK. You want to check an order you recently
received from Rossomon Skis from Mr/s Reynolds (Purchasing Department). Below are the details of the order, as they stand. Telephone
Student A.

Order No: 45688 Ski UK
Order: 600 white ski hats
　　　　450 leather ski gloves
Delivery date: 6.12.88
Price: ski hats − £1.50 per hat
　　　　ski gloves − £2.50 per pair
Payment terms: 30 days after delivery
Delivery point: Rossomon Skis UK Ltd
　　　　　　　　45 Sly Road
　　　　　　　　Uxbridge.

UNIT 10 **Job routines**

---

1. Listening ⬚

Tapescript

PJ: Oh, I usually get up about five, go for a jog before breakfast. We usually have
breakfast around 6.30. Then I have time to read the papers.

J: Which papers do you take?

PJ: Well, the *Financial Times, The Times* and *The Independent*. I don't exactly read them from cover to cover!

J: No, of course not.

PJ: Well, after the papers, I leave for the office. I'm usually behind my desk by 7.30. The first job of the day is the post. My secretary sorts out those letters which need immediate attention. Then round about 9.00, I have a daily meeting with Pete Sykes, he's my deputy. We run through the agenda for the day.

J: What's a typical day like?

PJ: Well, there's no such thing as a typical day, but I have regular morning meetings with my Finance and Sales Directors. Of course I travel abroad a lot, then I keep up to date by telephone.

J: What about lunch?

PJ: Well, I try to have lunch in the company canteen as often as possible. But, of course, sometimes I have lunch out with customers or the bank manager! People like that.

J: What about the afternoons?

PJ: If I'm in the country, I often go down to our plant and see how things are going. We have weekly management committee meetings on Friday afternoon. Then of course there are monthly board meetings, usually the first Monday of the month.

J: When do you finish work?

PJ: Round about seven. Then, if there's nothing on in the evening, I'll go home. More often than not, there's a dinner engagement. My wife comes to quite a lot of these, so at least we see each other.

J: When do you get to bed?

PJ: Rarely before midnight. I always read a book for half an hour before going to sleep.

J: Right, thank you Mr Johnson ...

Answers to the listening task

Events	Sequence
Visit the plant	10
Look at the post	6
Have breakfast	3
Meetings with Finance and Sales Directors	8
Read a book	14
Get up	1
Dinner engagement	13
Leave for the office	5
Go for a jog	2
Lunch in the canteen	9
Management/Board meetings	11
Read the newspapers	4
Meeting with deputy	7
Finish work	12
Go to sleep	15

3. Controlled practice

A (variations are possible)

A: *When do you get/wake up?*

B: Usually at six. At least my alarm clock goes off at six!
A: *Do you have breakfast straight away?*
B: No, I don't have breakfast straight away; first I go for a run.
A: *So, when do you sit down for/to have breakfast?*
B: I sit down for breakfast about seven.
A: *What do you do after breakfast?*
B: After breakfast I read the papers.
A: *Which papers do you read/take?*
B: Oh, the Guardian and the Independent.
A: *When do you leave for the office?*
B: I usually leave for the office about eight and I'm behind my desk by 8.30.
A: *What do you do first?*
B: I sort through the mail first.
A: *Do you have a secretary/Don't you have a secretary?*
B: No, I don't have a secretary. I wish I had!
A: *Do you usually stay in the office?*
B: No, usually I go out. Sometimes I even travel abroad.
A: *How often do you go/travel abroad?*
B: Oh, about four times a year. Usually to America.

B
1. I *occasionally* travel abroad./*Occasionally* I travel abroad.
2. I *often* have meetings.
3. I *sometimes* see the Managing Director./*Sometimes* I see the Managing Director.
4. I *hardly ever* see the Chairman.
5. I *always* catch the 7 o'clock bus.

UNIT 11 **Current projects**

1. Listening 🔊

MD: OK, let's have a look very briefly at the current departmental projects. Why don't we start with EDP? What are you working on at the moment?

EDP: We're doing a user study for the installation of the new micros. So we're talking to all the new users at the moment.

MD: Right, what about Finance? I believe you are thinking of changing our accounting system.

FM: Yes, that's right. We're having problems with the old system so we're looking into a new accounting system.

MD: Fine, let's move on to Marketing. Are you working on any special projects?

MM: Not really; but we are planning an advertising campaign for our new product.

MD: Interesting. I look forward to seeing it. What about Production?

PM: Well, as you know, we are currently installing the new automated assembly line.

MD: Of course. You must be pretty busy. Personnel, what are you doing?

PeM: We're trying to recruit new young graduates at the moment.

MD: How's that going?
PeM: Fine.
MD: Well, the Administration Department are not represented here today. They are moving to new offices next week, so they've got their hands full. Research and Development are also very busy — they're testing the new prototype. That just leaves Transport and Management Services. John?
TM: The Transport Department is rationalising the distribution network — so we're hoping for some big cost cuts in the near future.
MD: Good. And Management Services?
MSM: Well, we haven't got anything we're working on just at the moment but we are running a series of quality training seminars next month.
MD: Right, that just about covers it.

Answers to the listening task

Projects/fixed plans
Plan advertising campaign
Test new prototype
Move to new offices
Do user study
Rationalise distribution network
Run quality training seminars
Look into new accounting system
Try to recruit new graduates
Install automated assembly line

Departments
EDP Department
Finance Department
Marketing Department
Production Department
Personnel Department
Administration Department
Research and Development Department
Transport Department
Management Services Department

3. Controlled practice

MD: At the moment, the market *is expanding*. So this is an opportunity we must take. Our advertising agency *is working on* a new campaign for next month. Now, what about Production?
PM: Currently we *are running at* 75% capacity — so, that gives us some spare capacity.
MD: Good, how *are* we *doing on* staffing levels in the factory?
PM: We *are finding* it difficult to recruit technicians. There seems to be a shortage on the job market.
MD: What *are* you *planning* to do about it?
PM: Well, we *are thinking* of using a recruitment agency. A chap from a local agency *is coming* in to see me on Monday to talk about it.
MD: Fine, what about cash flow? This upturn in the market is going to be a drain on cash.
FM: That's right. At the moment, we *are managing* on an overdraft of about £50,000 and our current debts *are approaching* £85,000. I can go and talk to the Bank Manager about it. We've always been a good customer.
MD: Yes, do that as soon as possible. Finally, training. We're going to need some more sales reps and technicians in production. What *is happening* at the moment in training?
TM: We *are teaching* a refresher sales course but we've got spare capacity ...

Business correspondence 1

1. Listening 🔘

Tapescript

Call 1
A: I am phoning about the Birmingham contract.
B: Oh yes, how's it coming along?
A: Well, we've got problems with Petersons.
B: Really, what sort of problems?
A: They haven't delivered the cement.
B: Oh no. Why not?
A: No idea. Could you telex them?
B: Yes, of course, what's the order number?
A: It's PT4351 — Philipps is the contact man . . .

Call 2
A: I'm phoning about the spare parts we ordered.
B: Just a moment, I'll find the order form . . . that's strange, I can't find it anywhere. Can you give me the details?
A: Yes, we're waiting for 25 telecircuits and two microtesters — can't remember the order number.
B: When were you expecting delivery?
A: Well, last week we were told by 5 January.
B: Right, I'll have to look into it.
A: Can you telex me as soon as you have some news?
B: Of course, I'll do that.

Call 3
A: I'm phoning about the group of visitors from Australia.
B: Oh yes, have you got some details?
A: Well, a few — they're arriving on 5 November on Flight Number BA 456 . . . um . . . that's due in at half past two in the afternoon.
B: That sounds fine. Do you want me to pick them up?
A: That would be a great help. I'll confirm the details by telex.
B: Right, see you soon.
A: Bye.

Answers to listening task

Telex A: Telephone call 2
Telex B: Telephone call 3
Telex C: Telephone call 1

🔘

3. Controlled practice

A
1. Who is the telex sent to? *S. Jones*
2. Who is the telex from? *T. Bowden*
3. When will Mr Bowden be arriving at London Heathrow? *At 18.30 on 14 November.*
4. Will he take the underground from London Heathrow? *No, he will be picked up at the airport.*
5. When does he want to meet Mr Tomlinson? *At 09.30 on 15 November.*
6. Will he be staying in London for the whole trip? *No, he is also spending a day in Edinburgh.*
7. When will he be leaving? *At 10.30 on Friday 17 November.*
8. What does he want S. Jones to confirm by telex? *The appointment time with Mr Tomlinson.*

B
Suggested answers:
1. I would be grateful if you could confirm the receipt of my letter of 25 January.
   PLS CFM REC LTR DTD 25 JAN.
2. We apologise sincerely for the late delivery of part numbers 754 and 431.
   RGRT LATE DEL PART NOS 754 N 431.
3. I will meet you on 28 February next week at the Plaza Hotel. Could you please bring some samples of your work?
   MEET U 28 FEB PLAZA HOTEL. PLS BRING SMPLS UR WRK.
4. Thank you very much for the documents you sent me last week. I will get a reply to you as soon as possible.
   TKS DOCS SNT LST WK. WL RPLY ASAP.
5. We would like to inform you that we have recently moved to new premises.
   NB NEW ADDRSS.
6. I look forward to seeing you on 26 January.
   Yours sincerely
   J. Biggins
   SEE U 26 JAN.
   RGDS J BIGGINS

4. Transfer

Student B: You are Mr/s Müller at the Chamber of Commerce in Düsseldorf. Use the information below to reply to Student A's telex.

1. You are not allowed to give the names of personnel in companies. However, you can provide company names and addresses.
2. There is an annual electronics trade fair — ELECTRA. It takes place every year in Hannover. This year it will be held from 14—18 April. The address for further information is:
   ELECTRA FAIR
   Ludwigstrasse 28
   Hannover

Business correspondence 2

1. Listening

Tapescript

Call 1
A: I'm phoning about the letter I wrote to you.
B: Just a moment, I'll get it ... the one dated 15 November?
A: That's right. I asked for a quotation for a consultancy contract in December.
B: Yes, I see. Haven't we replied to it?
A: No, and as I said in the letter, we need it urgently.
B: Right, I'm sorry. I don't know why this has happened. I'll get back to you this afternoon.

Call 2
A: I'm phoning about the job advertised in *The Times* for the post of Office Manager.
B: Yes, have you put your application in writing?
A: Yes, I sent in my application two weeks ago.
B: Fine, then you'll be hearing from us in the near future.
A: I realise that. I just wanted to let you know my availability.
B: Right, go ahead.
A: Well, I can start the job from the beginning of April.
B: Right, I'll make a note of that but can you put it in writing?
A: Yes, of course. I'll get a letter in the post today.

Call 3
A: You know that hotel you recommended in your last letter?
B: Yes, you mean the one in Southern Italy?
A: Right. Well I've lost the letter and I wanted to book in for a couple of weeks this summer.
B: Just a moment, I'll see if I can find the address ... I'm sorry I can't find it.
A: Doesn't matter. Could you drop me a line?
B: Of course. I'll do that later this week.
A: Great. Nice talking to you. Bye.
B: Bye.

Answers to the listening task

Letter A: Telephone call 3
Letter B: Telephone call 1
Letter C: Telephone call 2

3. Controlled practice

Suggested answers

1. Dear Mr Phillips

   With *reference to* your letter of 10 August, *I am pleased to confirm* my participation at the International Sales Workshop in October.

   I would be grateful if you could send me details of the other participants and the programme. *Please find enclosed* some suggestions for contributions.

   I am afraid that I will not have the chance to see you before the workshop, but *I am looking forward* very much to meeting you in October.

   Yours *sincerely*

   P. Denton

   P Denton

2. *Subject:* Financial Audit

   Dear Sir

   I would be grateful if you could confirm that the dates of 21 to 23 June are convenient for the above-mentioned audit.

   I am afraid that Mr Howell will not be available; however, Mr Jenkins, one of our most experienced accountants *will do the audit*. He will be in touch direct concerning *his arrival* and other details.

   I would appreciate it if you could fax your draft accounts to us as soon as possible.

   Yours *faithfully*

   J. Svensson

   J Svensson
   Chief Auditor

4. Transfer

Model reply

Zacron Engineering
Unit 5
Hempstead Industrial Estate
Hemel Hempstead

Mr P Matthews
Technology in Engineering Conference
45 Broughton Street
Brighton

1 June 1988

Dear Mr Matthews

With reference to your letter of 25 May, I am pleased to *confirm my participation at this year's conference in July.*

I would be grateful *if you could send me further details about the programme.*

Unfortunately, *I will not be able to give an update on last year's talk.* I am afraid *that pressure of work will not allow time to prepare a talk.*

However, *I look forward to attending the conference again.*

Yours sincerely

JHiggins

J Higgins
Purchasing Manager

UNIT 14 Out and about

1. Listening 📼

Tapescript

Dialogue 1
A: Could you tell me how to get to __ __ __ __ __?
B: That's simple, turn left outside the station, walk down the road and under the wall.
A: Under the wall.
B: That's right, and then straight over Lendal Bridge and you'll see it in front of you, just at the end of Duncombe Place.
A: Right, I've got that. Thanks.
B: You're welcome.

Dialogue 2
A: Could you tell me how to get to __ __ __ __ __?
B: Of course. Turn left outside the station, go straight down and over Lendal Bridge. Then take the second right, that's Blake Street.
A: I'm sorry, I didn't get that last part.
B: Over the Bridge and then second right.
A: Fine, that's clear.
B: So, Blake Street leads into Davygate and you'll find it at the end on the left.
A: Right, thanks very much.
B: Bye.

Dialogue 3
A: Excuse me, could you tell me the way to __ __ __ __ __?
B: Yes, you go out of the station, turn left. Go straight ahead down Station Road. You'll come to the wall. Walk under the wall and then at the traffic lights left over Lendal Bridge.
A: Could you just go over that last part?
B: Of course, after the wall, turn left over Lendal Bridge.
A: Right.
B: Then take the first right after the Bridge and you'll see the building on your right.

A: I've got that. Thanks.
B: Pleasure. Bye.

Dialogue 4
A: Excuse me, could you tell me the quickest way to _ _ _ _ _?
B: Right, turn left outside the station. Follow the road down under the walls. Then go straight ahead down Rougier Street. Have you got that?
A: Yes, I think so.
B: The road leads into George Hudson Street. When you come to the traffic lights ...
A: I'm sorry. I didn't catch that last part.
B: Rougier Street leads into George Hudson Street. When you come to the traffic lights, turn left. Is that clear?
A: Yes.
B: Then walk over Ouse Bridge, then right at the junction and straight ...
A: Could you just go over that part?
B: Of course. Over Ouse Bridge, then right at the junction and then straight away left into Coppergate.
A: Over the Bridge, right and then first left?
B: That's right. Then you'll see it on your right.
A: OK. Thanks very much.
B: You're welcome. Bye.
A: Bye.

Answers to the listening task

a. 2
b. 4
c. 1
d. 3

---

3. Controlled practice

1. The way from the Minster (C3) to the cinema on Piccadilly (C2).

A: *Could you tell me the way* from the Minster to the cinema?
B: Yes, of course. *Walk down* Petergate into Low Petergate. *You'll see* the York College for Girls on your *left*.
A: York College for Girls on the left. *I've got that.*
B: Good. Continue down Low Petergate *until you come* to the junction with Goodramgate. *Have you got that?*
A: Yes.
B: At the junction go *straight across* and then down Colliergate. *When you reach* the junction with Pavement, turn *right* along Pavement.
A: *Could you just go over that last part?*
B: Yes. Walk down Colliergate and then right along Pavement.
A: *I've got that.*
B: Then *you'll come to* a junction with Parliament Street and Piccadilly. *Turn left* along Piccadilly and *you'll see* the cinema *on your* right.
A: Cinema on the right. OK, I think *I've got that.* Thanks very much.
B: You're welcome.

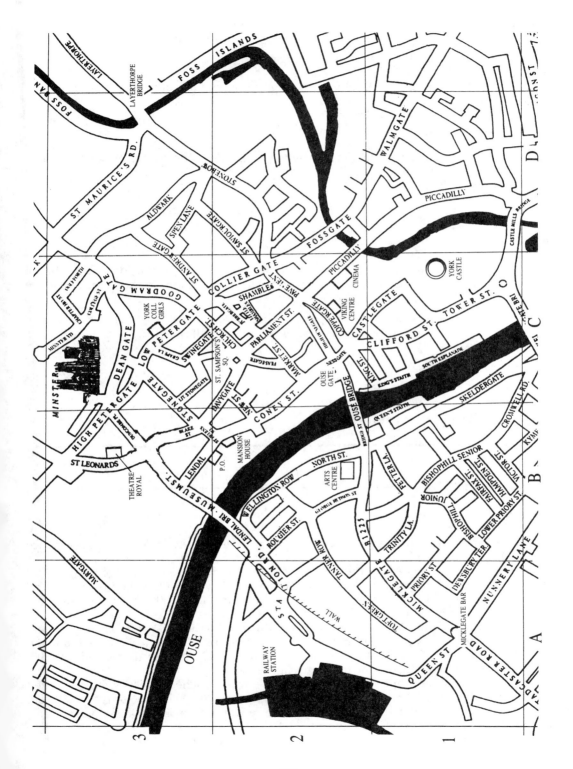

2. The way from York Castle (C1) to The Arts Centre (B2).

A: Could you tell me how *to get to the Arts Centre?*
B: Yes. *Walk down* Clifford Street *into* Nessgate.
A: Right. Down Clifford Street into Nessgate.
B: That's it. *At the junction* with Ousegate, *turn left* down Ousegate and then *walk across* the Ouse Bridge.
A: I'm sorry, *I didn't get that last part.*
B: Turn left and then walk over Ouse Bridge.
A: *I've got that.*
B: Good. *After* the Bridge, take *the first right* and *you'll see* the Arts Centre *on your left.*
A: First right after the Bridge and the Centre is *on my left.*
B: That's right. Bye.
A: Thanks, bye.

4. Transfer

PAIR WORK

Student B: You live in York. You are walking across Layerthorpe Bridge (D3) when a stranger (Student A) stops you and asks for directions to the Mansion House in St Helen's Square (B2).

Then ask Student A for directions from Micklegate Bar (A1) to the Theatre Royal. Make sure you understand and can follow all the directions.

UNIT 15 Sales review

1. Listening 📼

Tapescript

Before I go on to talk about sales targets for this year, let's have a look at the performance of our three main products over the last five years.

Let's start with the oldest — the AMAT. We launched this ten years ago and, as you can see, it reached its peak in 1983. The following two years, it levelled off at around 400,000. Then in 1986 and 1987 it decreased to a figure of 330,000 by the end of 1987. Finally, last year it fell to only 250,000 units.

OK, let's turn to the BMAT — we launched this product in 1982 and, as you can see, in the following three years, sales rose steadily to a peak of 550,000 in 1985. The following year it fell badly to 450,000. Then in 1987, it picked up again to settle around 500,000. In 1988, it remained constant at the same figure.

Finally, our most recent product — the CMAT — was launched in 1984. Sales increased rapidly in 1985 to reach 250,000 and then rose again by 200,000 in 1986 to reach 450,000. 1987 sales were also good — the end of year figure went up to 580,000. Last year's sales dropped slightly — they were down to 550,000.

OK, those are the results. Let's now look at some targets for 1989.

Answers to the listening task

Graph 1 — CMAT
Graph 2 — BMAT
Graph 3 — AMAT

3. Controlled practice

1. AMAT sales *reached a peak* in 1983.
2. In 1984 and 1985 the sales *levelled off* at 400,000.
3. In 1987 sales *fell* to 330,000.
4. In 1988 the figure *was* 250,000.
5. From 1983 to 1985, BMAT sales *rose* steadily to a *peak* of 550,000.
6. In 1986, sales *decreased/dropped* badly to 450,000.
7. In 1987 sales *levelled off* to settle at this figure.
8. In 1988 they *remained constant* at this figure.
9. CMAT sales *went up* rapidly in 1984 to *reach* 250,000.
10. In 1986, they *reached* 450,000.
11. In 1987 sales *increased* to 580,000.
12. In 1988 they *dropped/decreased* to 550,000.

4. Transfer

1. **Student B:** Listen to Student A's description of the performance of a product (sales and prices). As you listen, complete the graph below.

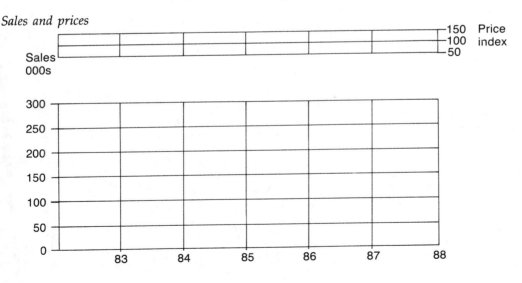

2. **Student B:** The graph below shows the performance of a product (turnover and profits). Describe it to Student A.

Turnover and profits

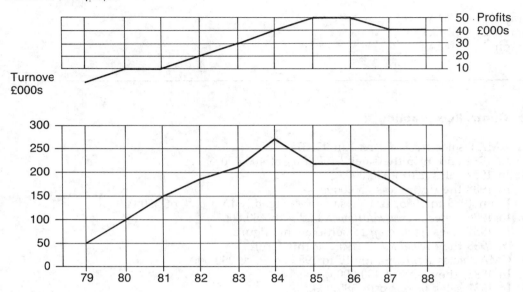

Sales forecasts

---

1. Listening 🔊 ─────────────────────────────────

Tapescript

Right, let's move on to the targets for 1989 and our medium-term plans. For the AMAT, we expect to reach sales of 250,000 — this is roughly the same figure as last year and it may be a little pessimistic, as we are going to do a large-scale promotion campaign during the year — so perhaps we will achieve something like 300,000. Still I prefer to keep the forecast at 250,000.

Now, we come to the BMAT. Here sales should reach 450,000. This could be a little optimistic as we are not going to push this product in 1989. In any case, the total will probably balance out with the more conservative forecast for the AMAT.

The CMAT, our most recent product, will continue to do well. Sales may go as high as 600,000. However, I have set the target slightly lower at 550,000.

OK, let's turn to our medium-term plans. At the beginning of 1989 we are going to launch our new product — the DMAT — and we are sure sales will take off very quickly. We estimate first year sales at 200,000. The DMAT should initially complement the AMAT and eventually replace it in the nineties.

Finally, R & D are working hard on a medium-range product — they hope to have it ready by 1990 so we could launch it in 1991.

Answers to the listening task

1. BMAT
2. DMAT
3. AMAT
4. CMAT

---

3. Controlled practice

1. BMAT sales will probably reach their target.
   We expect/think BMAT sales will reach their target.
2. I hope AMAT sales will be above target.
   AMAT sales could/may be above target.
3. We intend to launch the DMAT next year.
   The DMAT is going to be launched next year.
4. I am sure CMAT sales will reach their target.
   CMAT sales will (certainly)/are going to reach their target.
5. The DMAT should replace the AMAT.
   I expect/think the DMAT will replace the AMAT.
6. We hope our German subsidiary will launch a new medium-range product in 1991.
   Our German subsidiary could/may launch a new medium-range product in 1991.
7. The Sales team intend to carry out a large-scale promotion campaign.
   A large-scale promotion is going to be carried out by the Sales Team.
8. Total sales could be around £1,250,000 next year.
   I hope total sales will be around £1,250,000 next year.
9. I think the campaign will be successful.
   The campaign should/will probably be successful.
10. The R & D Department hope to have the product ready by 1990.
    The product may/could be ready by 1990.

4. Transfer

Student B: You are a supplier of office equipment. A customer (Student A) will telephone you about delivery dates. Use the information below to answer his/her questions. Use the language presented above to indicate the degree of likelihood.

Products	Delivery dates	Likelihood
office desks	10 June	probability
office chairs	30 May	certainty
calendars	1 July	possibility
year planners	30 October	probability
filing cabinets	7 August	certainty
security cupboards	1 September	possibility

When you have finished, compare your table with Student A's notes.

1. Listing 📼

Tapescript

I'd like to spend a few minutes of your time looking back over the year. I'm going to divide my review into three areas: firstly financial, secondly personnel and finally technology.

On the financial front, the results have been very pleasing. Turnover has increased by 14%, costs have dropped by 3% and profits are up by 16%. So the company as a whole has performed well. Some business areas have done better than others. Export sales have done very well — especially in America, our largest export market. The domestic consumer market has been very competitive and will continue to be so — our results in this market have been rather disappointing — just 1% up compared with last year.

Right, let's move on to personnel. Our policy of personnel development through training and promotion opportunities has continued to be a great success. We have actually recruited 72 new staff, while 20 have retired — so there's a net balance of 52. The training department has expanded considerably and moved into new areas such as quality assurance and sales training.

Finally technology. I thought you would be interested to have an update since this is vital for our future growth. Over the last year, our Research Department has thoroughly tested a new prototype engine. Results so far have looked promising. We have also invested heavily in a European technology programme which links industry with the universities.

Right, those are the three main areas — Finance, Personnel and Technology. Are there any questions, before I go on? . . .

Answers to the listening task

Three areas:
1. *Financial*   a. Results — turnover: + 14%
                                  — costs: − 3%
                                    — *profits*:   + 16%
               b. Exports: *Good esp. America*
                    Domestic consumer market: *very competitive, only 1% increase*
2. *Personnel*   a. Personnel Development
               b. Recruitment: *net increase 52*
               c. *Training*: has expanded
                    New areas: *quality* and *sales*
3. *Technology*   a. The Research Dept has tested prototype engine
               b. *Has invested in European Technology Programme*

3. Controlled practice

1. Turnover *increased* by 14% last year.
2. The company *has had* disappointing results recently.

3. The domestic consumer market *has been* very competitive.
4. Two years ago we *launched* an updated product.
5. We *have recruited* 20 junior managers.
6. *Have* you ever *visited* Australia?
7. We *went* there last June.
8. We *have* not *received* the results of the tests yet.
9. *Did* you *see* the report?
   Yes, it was interesting.
10. Three senior managers *have retired* this year.

4. Transfer
PAIR WORK
Student B: Student A is going to ask you a number of questions. Your answers should
be in either the present perfect or past simple.

UNIT 18 Company strategy

1. Listening

Tapescript

A: We need to define a new strategy but this strategy must be flexible enough to take
account of changing market conditions.
B: I agree. Our main objective must be to gain market share, and to do this we must
reduce prices.
A: So are you sure that if we reduce prices, our market share will increase?
B: Yes, I'm sure.
C: That's probably true, but if we reduce prices, our margins will be lower and that will
cut profits.
B: In the short term that's right, but we can slowly increase production, and with increased
production, we'll cut unit costs.
C: That's really a long-term prospect. Unit costs can only come down if we invest in new
plant and machinery.
A: Let's stop there a minute and try to define our strategy in two directions — firstly
the market and secondly manufacturing. Do we agree that increased market share is
the objective?
C: No, I don't agree. I think we should go for higher profitability. If we can upgrade
the product, we'll get better prices and therefore higher profits.
B: Look, the market is already very competitive and getting more so. If we increase prices,
whatever the quality, sales will drop rapidly.
A: Right, let's look at it from the other point of view — manufacturing.
C: Well, if we can reduce costs in manufacturing, that must put us in a strong position
to adapt to the market. The only way we can be flexible enough is to sub-contract
more of the production.
B: But it'll mean job losses if we do that.
C: Yes, but the jobs that remain will be more secure.

Answers to the listening task

1. d	5. g
2. e	6. c
3. a	7. h
4. f	8. b

3. Controlled practice

Suggested answers:

1. Our customers will be more satisfied
   We will have more satisfied customers · if we improve the delivery service.
2. If we rationalise production, unit costs will be reduced.
3. There will be job losses
   We will have job losses · if we rationalise production.
4. If we install robots, our labour costs will be lower.
   we will lower our labour costs.
5. There will be a price war
   We will have a price war · if competitors enter the market.
6. We can/will charge higher prices if we upgrade the product.
7. We can/will earn larger profits if we increase our margins.
8. If we do no research · there will be no new products.
   If we don't do any research · there won't be any new products.
9. If we don't offer better salaries, we won't attract the best people.
10. If there are fewer meetings
    If we have fewer meetings · we will have more time to do our jobs.

4. Transfer

Student B: Answer Student A's questions like this:

If my company moves to another location, I will ...

Then think up some 'If' questions to ask Student A.

UNIT 19 Competition

1. Listening

Tapescript

Let's look at the competition. Now, our main competitor — Benton — entered the market in 1982 — ten years later than us. But since then they have grown more rapidly and are now the biggest in terms of market share. Why? Mainly because of their product development. Their products are better, sold at lower prices and presented more attractively. At the moment their main weakness is that they have the lowest profitability.

Now our second major competitor is Zecron. They entered the market at the same time as us. They have a lower market share than us and their products are sold at slightly higher prices. However, their annual return shows greater profitability and much heavier investment in plant and machinery over the last two years. So they are in a good position to overtake us soon.

The last competitor is Mansell. They have been in the market slightly longer than us and Zecron. They have a much smaller market share, but their products are sold at the top end of the market at much higher prices. As a result they achieve the best profitability of the four companies with much lower turnover.

So, what can we say about our own position? Well, our products are medium-price but less attractive than Benton's. We're getting a problem with reliability. Certainly Benton's range has a reputation for being much more reliable. Our market share is higher than Zecron and Mansell, but they are more profitable than us. So, we must become more competitive during the next two years if we are to hold on to our market share and increase profitability.

Answers to the listening task

	Age in market 1 = oldest	Market share	Product price 1 = cheapest	Profitability 1 = most profitable
Brotherton	2	2	2	3
Benton	4	1	1	4
Zecron	2	3	3	2
Mansell	1	4	4	1

3. Controlled practice

1. Mansell have been in the market *the longest*.
2. Brotherton entered the market *earlier* than Benton.
3. Benton entered the market ten years *later* than Brotherton.
4. Benton have *the largest/biggest* market share.
5. Mansell have a much *smaller/lower* market share than Brotherton.
6. Benton's products are sold at *the lowest* prices.
7. Mansell's products are sold at *much higher* prices than Brotherton's.
8. Zecron's products are *slightly more expensive* than Brotherton's.
9. Mansell is *the most* profitable company.
10. Brotherton is *more profitable* than Benton.

4. Transfer

Student B: Use the table below to answer Student A's questions. Answer like this:

129

_ _ _ _ _ is the most _ _ _ _ _.
_ _ _ _ _ _ is more _ _ _ _ _ _ than _ _ _ _ _ _.

Company	Turnover	Profitability	Share capital	Employees
Cittabank	1	2	1	4
RA Chemicals	2	1	3	1
Elton Oil	4	3	2	3
Natelecom	3	4	4	2

UNIT 20 Stock control

1. Listening 🔘

Tapescript

A: Let's go through the inventory then. Let's start with fuel — first liquid gas?
B: We've got about 200 litres. The recommended stock level is 400.
A: So we've got too little. Better put an order in. The other fuel is coal for the furnace?
B: About 50 tons. Recommended level is 30.
A: A bit too much then — run the stocks down over the next week. Now then, what about spare parts? We're always running short of cable.
B: Let me just see what we've got ... about 30 metres in stock.
A: Is that enough?
B: No, maybe a bit too little. I'll order some more.
A: What about pipes?
B: Well, we've got 25. That's plenty. Probably too many.
A: OK. Now let's move on to the packing material. First, boxes?
B: About 400 in stock — too few I think for this time of year. I'll put them on order.
A: And how much wrapping paper are we carrying?
B: About one ton. Slightly too little.
A: OK. And how many pallets for stacking?
B: That's a problem. We've had difficulties getting them back. We've far too few at the moment.
A: Um ... we'll have to do something about that.

Answers to the listening task

Item	too much	too little	too many	too few
liquid gas		X		
coal	X			
cable		X		
pipes			X	
boxes				X
paper		X		
pallets				X

3. Controlled practice

A.

table (C)	diary (C)
office (C)	equipment (U)
furniture (U)	ink (U)
telephone (C)	wisdom (U)
information (U)	personnel (U)
screen (C)	person (C) – people
advice (U)	wife (C) – wives
data (U)	safety (U)
news (U)	newspaper (C)
service (C)	paper (U)
sale (C)	security (U)

(NOTE: securities (C) = shares)

B.
1. How *much* time have you got?
2. I'm sorry, I've only got a *little* money on me.
3. I can't give you *much* advice, I'm afraid.
4. I'll ring you back in a *few* minutes.
5. How *many* times have you been here?
6. I've only got a *few* coins, no notes.
7. There isn't *much* news today.
8. We shouldn't use so *much* paper now the computer is installed.
9. I like rooms with just a *little* furniture.
10. We've far too *many* items in stock.

4. Transfer

Student B: You run a restaurant with Student A. You are doing a stock check. Student A
will ask you questions about the stock levels of the following items. Answer
like this:

We've got _____ kilos/cans — too much/many/few/little.

+ = *overstocked*
− = *understocked*

Items:

flour	30 kilos (−)	red house wine	25 bottles (−)
sugar	59 kilos (+)	white house wine	45 bottles (+)
salt	5 kilos (+)	perrier water	30 bottles (−)
pepper	1 kilo (+)	orange juice	10 packets (−)
tomatoes	3 kilos (−)	cans of beer	30 cans (+)
lettuces	10 (−)	bottles of coke	50 (−)
spaghetti	10 packets (−)	beef	5 kilos (+)
salami	500 gms (−)	cans of tomatoes	10 (+)
fruit	5 kilos (−)	strawberries	2 punnets (−)

UNIT 21 Project timing

1. Listening 📼

Tapescript

A: I'm phoning about the timing for the Vienna project.
B: Right, we've got a starting date for that, haven't we?
A: Yes, we begin a pilot study on 5 November.
B: Right, how long is that expected to last?
A: We should finish the study in three weeks.
B: Good, then what's the next stage?
A: Well, we've got a meeting with the contractor scheduled for 1 December. If everything
goes according to plan, we'll sign the contract then. And work can begin at the
beginning of January.
B: So what's the first stage?
A: Well, excavation will begin in January and is due to finish by the middle of February.
Now, after that we could have a problem.
B: What's that?
A: You remember we've sub-contracted the German firm to do the foundations. They
promised to start in the middle of February. They are now saying they can't.
B: Right, I'll get on to them. When are they due to finish the foundations?
A: In the contract, it says by 28 February.
B: I see, and then?

A: Construction work should begin on 5 March. We're on a pretty tight schedule. All the work has to be done in March and April.

B: OK. I see the problem. I'll phone you back in the afternoon at about three. Bye.

A: Goodbye.

Answers to the listening task

Key:

1. ▦ — Pilot study

2. X — Meeting with contractors

3. ▬ — Excavations

4. ▒ — Foundations

5. ▨ — Construction

---

3. Controlled practice

1. The work is due to begin *at/by* the end of April.
2. We are hoping to meet the engineer *at* the weekend.
3. We expect to sign the contract sometime *in* June.
4. We arrived *in* time to see them leave.
5. They are scheduled to finish *by/in* the middle of July.
6. I arranged to meet him *at* 15.30 *on* Tuesday.
7. The plane took off precisely *on* time.
8. We are busiest *in* spring.
9. The contract must be finalised *by* the end of the month.
10. He phoned me *at* 1 o'clock *at* night.

4. Transfer

Student B: Use the project planner below to answer Student A's questions.

Key:

1. Preliminary study   ▦

2. Contract negotiation   X

3. Feasibility study   ▬

4. Training   ▒

5. Installation   ▨

6. Implementation date   O

Project Planner

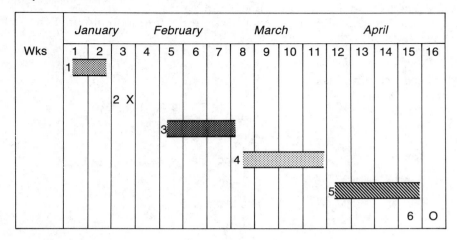

UNIT 22 Factory tour

1. Listening 🔘

Tapescript

Right. Basically there are three parts of the plant — the supply area, the assembly area and the despatch area.

So let's start here in the supply area. The raw materials come by truck and are off-loaded onto a conveyor. The conveyor takes them into the supply room. As you can see, this room is divided into three storage areas. On the shelves we store the electronic components. Stacked up against the wall are the boards and between the boards and the shelves we store the chemicals used in the process.

Right, let's go through into the assembly area. In this first part, the boards are cut into shape. There is one passing through the cutter now and then holes are drilled into the board ... the boards come out of the drilling machine and then the components are inserted into the holes. If we go across to the other side, you'll see the boards coming off a conveyor.

So the assembled boards then go into the despatch area, which is behind this door. The boards are sorted according to their type and size over here — on this big table. Then they are stacked in front of this table here. And finally they are packed in boxes ready for despatch.

Answers to the listening task

1. c   9. g
2. a   10. i

3. e	11. m
4. b	12. o
5. d	13. l
6. h	14. k
7. j	15. n
8. f	

3. Controlled practice

1. London lies *on* the River Thames.
2. I'll meet you *in* the airport.
3. I'll meet you *at* the airport.
4. I can't find Tweedale Street at all. It must be *off* the map.
5. Cologne is *between* Bonn and Düsseldorf.
6. We walked *through* the main hall to the conference room.
7. My car is parked *in front of* the building.
8. Where's Peter? He just walked *out of* the office.
9. Come *into* my office. We can talk in private there.
10. On a clear day, you can see *across* the Channel *to* France.
11. Now I remember the bridge. It's *over* the River Avon.
12. Exhausted after the meeting, he dropped his briefcase *onto* the desk.
13. He put the document *in/into* the safe.
14. I took the letter *out of* the filing cabinet.
15. The ship sails *from* Hamburg *to* Stockholm.
16. The tunnel will be built 100 metres *below* sea level.

4. Transfer
PAIR WORK

Student B: Use the plan below to tell Student A where the furniture is located in the office.

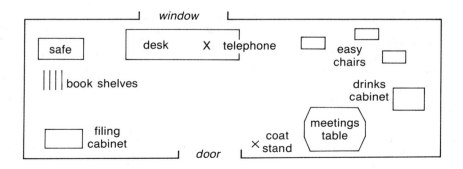

UNIT 23 **Market research**

1. Listening 🔘

Tapescript

A: Right. I'd just like to check some details first. It's Mr and Mrs J. Reynolds, isn't it?
B: Yes.
A: The address is 21 Pine Avenue?
B: Yes.
A: Your telephone number is 56822, is that right?
B: No, it's 56882.
A: Thanks. Now I hope you don't mind if I ask you some personal questions?
B: No, go ahead.
A: First, do you own this house?
B: Yes, we do.
A: How many people live in it?
B: Well there's myself, my husband and two sons.
A: So four of you. Where does your husband work?
B: He works at Courtaulds.
A: And do you work?
B: No, I'm at home.
A: Right, your sons are at school then?
B: Yes, that's right.
A: Do they go to the local school?
B: No, they both go into town to the Independent Boys School.
A: Now, both you and your husband have a car?
B: Yes, we do.
A: Roughly how many miles do you do a year?
B: Well, about 5,000.
A: Your husband's car is on the firm, is that right?
B: Yes.
A: How many holidays a year do you take?
B: Normally two.
A: In this country or abroad?
B: Usually a summer holiday abroad and a week somewhere in England in the autumn.
A: Somewhere by the sea?
B: No, we normally go to Scotland walking.
A: Right, just a couple more questions; then I'm finished. Do you mind telling me how much you normally spend on your summer holiday?
B: Well I suppose about £1,000.
A: And this year you plan to go abroad?
B: Yes, Greece actually.
A: Well, thank you very much, Mrs Reynolds. You've been very helpful.
B: You're welcome.

Answers to the listening task

1. The consumer is called Mrs J. Reynolds.   T

2. She lives at 21 Pine Avenue.   T
 3. Her telephone number is 56822.   F
 4. They rent their house.   F
 5. Four people live in the house.   T
 6. Both Mr and Mrs Reynolds work.   F
 7. Her sons go to the local school.   F
 8. They have two cars.   T
 9. She drives about 5,000 miles a year.   T
10. They take two foreign holidays a year.   F
11. They usually go to the sea.   F
12. They spend about £1,000 on their summer holiday.   T
13. They plan to go to Greece this year.   T

---

3. Controlled practice

 1. Your name is P. Thomas, isn't it?
 2. Your address is 45 Main Street (isn't it/is that right)?
 3. And you own your house (don't you/is that right)?
 4. Where do you work?
 5. Have you worked there for long?
 6. How do you travel/get to work?
 7. Do you have any children?
 8. How old are they?
 9. Are they at school?
10. What do they do in the evenings?
11. How often do you go to the cinema?
12. Do you ever go to restaurants?
13. When do you go to bed?

UNIT 24 The budget meeting

1. Listening

Tapescript

P: Right, let's get started. Now, you've all seen the budget proposals for next year. Have you got anything to say?
J: I think the research figure is too low. We should increase it by at least 5%.
P: Well, we could do that, but it means less money for the other departments. I think it should stay the same.

s: I agree with John. We could reduce the figure for marketing — that would allow us to increase the budget for research.
P: I felt marketing needed a good figure this year. They've got a big launch mid-year. I think they couldn't manage with less.
J: I'm sure they could and ...
P: Just a moment. Let's look at the other two department budgets. That's production and sales.
J: Well, we can't cut the production budget, that's for sure. I don't know about sales.
s: Why do you say we can't cut production's budget? They had a big investment last year. Well, surely they could manage on less this year?
P: Yes, I think I agree. Production ought to manage with less this year, having spent so much last year.
s: A small cut in the production budget might mean we could increase the research figure.
P: Right, I'll put that to the Production Manager. Finally, what about sales?
s: I think it's a bit high. They might save a bit by spending less on the after-sales side.
P: John, any views?
J: Well, I think we should spend more on sales.
P: That's out of the question. The figure shouldn't be changed.

Answers to the listening task

Budget proposals

Departments	Budget	Peter	John	Susan
Research	£25,000	OK	+	+
Marketing	£45,000	OK	−	−
Production	£145,000	−	OK	−
Sales	£55,00	OK	+	−

3. Controlled practice

 1. We *should/ought to reduce the sales budget.*
 2. Marketing *might accept a cut in their budget.*
 3. We *can't cut the production budget.*
 4. We *could spend more on direct sales activities.*
 5. We *should/ought to reduce the total budget.*
 6. Research *can't continue on this budget.*
 7. More money *could be made available.*
 8. We *shouldn't/ought not to cut the Marketing budget.*
 9. Sales *might not reach their target.*
10. Production *could need more money later in the year.*

1. Listening

Tapescript

MD: There's no doubt we've got to tighten up on financial control. Peter, you're in charge of credit control. What do you suggest?

FC: Well, I've been looking at our payment terms — in other words how long we have to wait for payment — we must reduce the average delay in payment. It's nearly 45 days now from the date we send out the invoice. We've got to get it down to near 30 days. It's not easy. The Sales people always argue it is better to wait for payment rather than lose a customer, but I think we can tighten up on reminders, statements and so on.

MD: What about our payments to suppliers?

FC: Well, that's more difficult. We are a small firm dealing with large suppliers. They don't have to help us. Still, maybe one or two of our older suppliers could give us better payment terms.

MD: Right, let's look at some more general cost-cutting measures we can take. I'm interested in support services such as training and personnel development.

PM: Look, I must say something here. We simply mustn't cut these services. They are our long-term investment in people.

MD: Maybe, but we've got to reduce costs somehow. We can't cut in the production area. I . . .

PM: True, but our training budget is already very limited. Most of the training programmes are long term.

MD: I'm not saying we have to stop any existing programmes, but perhaps we should look carefully at future training courses.

PM: Well, I can let you have details of what we plan. I think you'll see that they are all worthwhile investments.

MD: I'm sure. Anyway, let me have the programme and we'll discuss it later. We'll have to stop now. I've got another meeting at 2.

PM: I must go too. I've got a meeting straight away.

Answers to the listening task

Statements	*T/F*
The MD feels they must tighten up on financial control.	T
The Financial Controller feels they have got to reduce payment times.	T
They must reduce payment times to 30 days.	T
They must get tough with their customers.	F
Their suppliers must help them.	F
The Personnel Manager feels they don't have to cut training and personnel development.	F
The Managing Director feels they must reduce costs.	T
The Managing Director feels they have got to stop some existing training.	F

Both the Managing Director and the Personnel Manager have to leave for
  other meetings.   T

3. Controlled practice

1. We mustn't expand too fast.
2. We don't have to/needn't enter export markets yet.
3. We've got to/We must/We have to discuss this at the next meeting.
4. We have to/We've got to fire him.
5. We don't have to pay the Christmas bonus.
6. We mustn't enter this part of the building.
7. We must/We have to/We've got to leave now.
8. We don't have to/needn't catch that plane.
9. We mustn't miss the 18.00 plane.
10. We must/We have to/We've got to increase our turnover.

Telex appendix

Abbreviation	Meaning
ADD	Addition
ADV	Advise
APP	Appointment
ARR	Arrive
ARRNG	Arrange
ARRVL	Arrival
APPROX	Approximate(ly)
ASAP	As soon as possible
ATTN	Attention
CFM	Confirm
CHNG	Change
CO	Company
DEL	Deliver(y)
DEP	Depart(ure)
DLY	Delay
DOC	Document
ENCL	Enclosed
ESP	Especially
FAO	For the attention of
FLT	Flight
INFM	Inform
INFO	Information
INV	Invoice
LST	Last
LTR	Letter
MAX	Maximum
MGR	Manager
MIN	Minimum
MTG	Meeting
N	And
NB	Please note
NO	Number
NXT	Next
OBT	Obtain
OK	Agreement
OK?	Do you agree?
ORD	Order
OURLET	Our letter
OURTELCON	Our telephone conversation
PLS	Please
POSS	Possible
RE	Reference/About
REC	Received/Receipt

RGDS	Regards
RGRT	Regret
RPLY	Reply
THKS	Thanks
TLX	Telex
U	You
UR	Your
VST	Visit
WK	Week
WL	Will
WRK	Work

Vocabulary Index